MARY

in Different
Traditions

*Seeing the
Mother of Jesus
with New Eyes*

Thomas G. Casey, SJ

Paulist Press
New York / Mahwah, NJ

First published 2019 by Messenger Publications, Dublin, Ireland
Designed by Messenger Publications Design Department
Cover images: Shutterstock: AjayTvm, Anna Davidovskaya,
FotograFFF, Gouache7 and Wikimedia images public domain.
Typeset in Adobe Caslon Pro
Printed by Hussar Books

Library of Congress Cataloging-in-Publication Data is available upon request.

ISBN 978-0-8091-5513-2 (Paperback)

Published in North America by Paulist Press
997 Macarthur Boulevard
Mahwah, New Jersey 07430
www.paulistpress.com

CONTENTS

DEDICATION

To Rachel, Rebecca, Sarah, Joshua, Thomas and David.
Thanks for helping me see that she's the cause of our joy.

INTRODUCTION

*Imagining Mary in words and pictures has always been
one of the most powerful ways of imagining the Church,
and so of imagining ourselves freshly.*

Rowan Williams, former Archbishop of Canterbury

Did you know that?
+ Mary, the mother of Jesus, is the only woman mentioned by name in the Koran or Qur'an. Her name appears more often in the holy book of Islam than in the entire New Testament.
+ Martin Luther, the leading figure of the Protestant Reformation, wrote one of the masterpieces of world Marian literature after his break with the Catholic Church.
+ Mary was brought up Jewish, not Catholic.

This last point is intentionally provocative, but there is a serious side to it also. Although most Catholics know that Mary wasn't brought up Catholic, in practice many Catholicss relate to her as though she had always been Catholic and nothing else. The first two points show that Mary is more alive and well in the non-Catholic world than many Catholics realise. Indeed, at times, Mary is actually more revered outside the Catholic fold than within it.

Catholics regard Mary as a good woman who lived a good life. But beyond that, most don't have a lot to say about her. Although some Catholics are devoted to her, others simply respect her and still others remain benignly indifferent, because the question of Mary is not an issue for them, but a non-issue.

Over the last sixty years or so, Catholics, at least in the Western world, have moved from a situation where Marian devotion was simply taken for granted to a new situation where it now demands a real effort to turn to Our Lady in any meaningful way. Nowadays, Catholics are more likely to carry iPods rather than Rosary beads, and to sport a tattoo instead of wearing the miraculous medal. It's a sea change, and yet it has happened without fanfare, almost without our noticing it, 'off stage', as the late Irish poet Seamus Heaney would have put it.

The trouble is not simply that we have stopped thinking about Mary in the way our ancestors did, but that we no longer feel about her in the same way they did either. Fundamentally, we have lost our ability to marvel about Mary. If she no longer elicits a sense of wonder in us, we'll be tempted to dismiss devotion to her as a waste of time.

How can we learn to see Mary in a new way? Instead of using the resources of our long Catholic tradition, which, despite their indisputable worth, can come across as somewhat hackneyed, in this book I'd like to take a different approach. I'd like to explore the insights of other traditions and faiths – Lutheranism, Orthodoxy, Islam and Judaism.

I will explore these other perspectives not so much at the doctrinal level, but at the level of their experiences of Mary, the stories they tell about her and – in the case of Judaism – the stories told about similar kinds of women to Mary. It will be an imaginative exploration rather than a systematic study. Perhaps the novelty of their viewpoints on Mary can bring us to the joy of surprise about her once again. If we can learn to wonder anew about this woman from Nazareth, maybe we'll be brought to enjoy the even greater wonder of her son, Jesus.

Marian Insights in Unexpected Places

I used to think there was little I could learn about Mary from those outside the Catholic world. After all, with the exception of the Orthodox world, where she plays a truly significant role, she is at best marginal. The various Protestant Churches respect Mary but don't always embrace her with enthusiasm; she has a minor role in Islam; and she is hardly ever mentioned by those of the Jewish faith. However, when I began to explore what other traditions and faiths have to say about Mary, it began to dawn on me how wrong I was. There is a treasure trove of Marian insights, not only among Christians of other traditions, but also in Judaism and Islam, insights that can help us see her with new eyes.

Let me just give you a preview of what is coming by briefly mentioning how these various traditions help us to see Mary from a fresh viewpoint.

Luther and the Lutheran Tradition
Martin Luther, Ulrich Zwingli and John Calvin stand out as the three leading reformers. All of them regarded Mary as the Mother of God. They believed in her virginity and freedom from sin. But each of them also emphasised that she must be always kept subordinate to Christ,

and should not be looked on as a mediator. After their deaths, from the late sixteenth century onwards, attitudes toward Mary took a downward turn among most of the Reformed churches. The sole exception was the Church of England. To this day, the Virgin Mary continues to be held in high esteem by Anglicans.

The chapter will begin by looking at a masterpiece of Marian literature, written by none other than Martin Luther, the iconic figure of the Protestant Reformation. Precisely at the time he was definitively breaking from Rome, Luther was hard at work composing a beautiful commentary on Mary's *Magnificat*. Together with Luther, we will ask: how can we sing the Magnificat with Mary, how can we be grateful with her? Luther shows us how we can identify with Mary by emphasising what makes her similar to us, rather than stressing what sets her apart. Then I'll turn to two later Lutheran figures, Søren Kierkegaard and Dietrich Bonhoeffer. Kierkegaard, the prophetic nineteenth-century Lutheran thinker, shows us how we can grow in faith and cope with anxiety by following the example of Mary. Bonhoeffer, the twentieth-century Lutheran pastor and theologian who was executed by the Nazis, highlights the power and forcefulness of Mary's Magnificat.

Orthodoxy
The huge emphasis on liturgical prayer in the Orthodox world shapes its view of Mary. She is especially present in the chanted prayer of the liturgy and in the icons which adorn Orthodox churches. Compared to Roman Catholics, Orthodox Christians give less emphasis to doctrines and theology concerning Mary, and much more weight to the felt experience of revering Mary through hymns, icons and the common prayer of the liturgy. In the chapter on Mary and Orthodox Christianity, I will focus on Mary as a living icon of God and on her decisive role in the spirituality of Orthodoxy.

Judaism
Since those of the Jewish faith don't believe that Jesus was the Messiah, most have no interest in his mother Mary, and so they have nothing to say about her. The few who do have something to say about Mary see her at best as just another Jewish mother. So, rather than take my starting point from nothing – this noticeable silence concerning Mary – I'll instead explore how we as Catholics can deepen our understanding of Mary by

reminding ourselves of a simple truth that we often overlook: Mary was Jewish. She was Jewish in two important ways: first, she belonged to the Jewish people; second, she grew up in the Jewish faith. So her Judaism was both ethnic and religious. In the chapter on Mary and Judaism, I will look at Mary's Jewish faith, at how she is already prefigured in the Old Testament, and at what it meant for Mary to be part of the chosen people, and to feel herself chosen by God.

Islam

Muslims are not Christians, so we shouldn't be taken aback if their beliefs about Mary differ significantly from ours. But the surprising thing is that we actually have much in common. Let's get the big difference out in the open first: Islam doesn't regard Jesus as the Son of God, and so Muslims refuse to call Mary God's mother. God is utterly transcendent, and so they object to linking him too closely to any creature. Giving Mary the exalted title of Mother of God appears to them like a violation of the transcendence that is proper to God alone. However, on the positive side, there is an extraordinary warmth and reverence in the way Mary is portrayed in the holy book of Islam, the Qur'an. The depiction of Mary in the Qur'an will be the focus of the first part of the chapter on Mary and Islam. The second part will go on to look at what role Mary could play in dialogue between Catholics and Muslims.

I am confident you'll find food for thought in these pages. By the end I hope you'll see how Mary has an appeal that extends far beyond the Catholic tradition. The discovery of new ways of seeing Mary has made her more alive for me; I hope this happens for you as well.

CHAPTER ONE

MARY *in* LUTHER
and the LUTHERAN TRADITION

*She became the Mother of God, in which work so many and such great
good things are bestowed on her as pass man's understanding. For on
this there follows all honour, all blessedness, and her unique place in
the whole of mankind, among which she has no equal, namely, that she
had a child by the Father in heaven, and such a child.*

Martin Luther

There has been much constructive dialogue between Anglicans and
Roman Catholics about Mary and her role, and both are in agreement on
the core principles concerning devotion to the Mother of God. However,
this chapter won't analyse any official pronouncements about Mary. Such
pronouncements are certainly important. But the primary (though not
exclusive) aim of this book is to help Catholics rediscover Mary, and the
real struggle we Catholics have with the figure of Mary is not at the
theoretical level, but at the level of our feelings and attitudes. It's not that
we dislike her; it's more that she has become less and less real for us. We
find it difficult to see her as someone to whom we can relate in a genuine
and unforced way. Examining a series of doctrinal statements won't
unblock this affective impediment, because theoretical analysis doesn't
speak to the heart. However, Martin Luther, Søren Kierkegaard and
Dietrich Bonhoeffer could just stir us up. That's because they write about
Mary with feeling and fervour. Since the Bible plays such a central role
in the Reformed Churches, these three passionate Christians concentrate
on Mary's portrayal in Scripture. They challenge us to base our devotion
to Mary upon a solidly biblical foundation.

Mary in Martin Luther's Magnificat
The years 1520 and 1521 marked a turbulent period in the life of Martin
Luther. In June 1520, Pope Leo X issued the bull *Exsurge Domine* ('Arise,

Oh Lord'), declaring that forty-one statements in Luther's Ninety-five Theses were heretical, and threatening Luther with excommunication if he did not recant his teaching. The bull took four months to get to Luther, only arriving in Wittenberg on 10 October 1520. Luther was given sixty days to decide how to respond. On 10 December 1520 he responded in a public manner that left no room for ambiguity: gathering with supporters in Wittenberg, he threw the papal bull into a blazing bonfire. This led, on 3 January 1521, to the bull that officially excommunicated him, marking his definitive break with Rome.

Yet despite all these tumultuous events, Luther did not neglect writing or study. We know from one of his letters that as early as November 1520, he was already at work writing a commentary on Mary's canticle of praise, the Magnificat. We can gauge something of the importance of this task for Luther by noting that even being excommunicated didn't put him off this project so dear to his heart. He only interrupted his writing in April 1521 in order to attend the Diet of Worms. Although this sounds like a particularly unappetising series of meals, it was in fact an assembly (Diet) in a German town (Worms)! Luther had been summoned there either to retract or reassert his new teachings. He arrived on 16 April 1521, and for the next two days bravely defended his views. On his way home from Worms, as he travelled through the Black Forest, he was intercepted by masked horsemen. They pretended to kidnap Luther, but it later emerged that the whole event had been staged by his protector Prince Frederick III, Elector of Saxony, in an effort to save Luther from those who may have been really intent on putting an end to his life.

Luther was kept in hiding in Wartburg Castle for the next ten months or so. He called Wartburg Castle his 'Patmos', referring to the island where Saint John the Evangelist is traditionally said to have composed the Book of Revelation. It was while he was in seclusion there that he resumed his commentary on Mary's Magnificat, completing it in June 1521. When the book was published a few months later, Pope Leo X, the very person who had excommunicated him, declared after reading it: 'Blessed are the hands that have written this.'

Luther's commentary on the Magnificat is dedicated to a young nobleman, John Frederick I, the Elector of Saxony. Although only eighteen years of age when the commentary was completed, John Frederick was already in correspondence with Luther and had become one of his most avid supporters. As a mark of gratitude for all the support he received from John Frederick, Luther dedicated this heartfelt commentary to his enthusiastic teenage admirer.

Gratitude is also a theme that stands out in Luther's study of Mary's Magnificat, and we Catholics can learn much from Luther's insights into Mary's spirit of thankfulness. Luther maintains that Mary did not sing the Magnificat for herself alone, but also for us, in order that we could learn to sing it, and like Mary, to praise and thank God for his goodness. Luther divides the Magnificat into two main parts. In the first part, Mary rejoices in the gifts she has received from God in her own life. In the second part, she gives thanks for what God has done in human history as a whole. As he goes through each part of the Magnificat, Luther comments on Mary's canticle line by line. Let's see for ourselves how Luther highlights Mary's fundamental disposition of gratitude.

The first line of the Magnificat is 'My soul magnifies the Lord'. Instead of saying 'I', Mary uses the words 'my soul'. Luther notes that in the Bible the words 'soul' and 'life' are often synonymous. So, when Mary declares that her soul magnifies the Lord, she is effectively saying that all of her life is given over to loving and praising God. Mary is filled with the Holy Spirit, and the joy she feels is a sure sign that God is at work in her. According to Luther, the fact that Mary 'magnifies' God, is a clear indication that her hymn is about 'the great works and deeds of God'. As a grateful person, her attention is not centred on herself, but upon God, towards whom she is filled with gratitude. He contrasts Mary with 'two kinds of false spirits that cannot sing the Magnificat' in the right way. First, there are the people who will only thank and praise God when things are going well for them. As soon they encounter any problems, they stop singing and lose all respect for God. The second group is worse still, because instead of thanking God for his gifts, these people want to be honoured as though these gifts were their own possessions. Tragically, God's gifts end up making them proud and complacent, and they begin to sing a different kind of song: My soul magnifies me! As for Mary, 'she does not desire herself to be esteemed; she magnifies God alone and gives all glory to him'.

In the second line Mary says, 'my spirit rejoices in God, my Saviour'. Luther notes that Mary rejoices first of all in God. She calls him God before calling him Saviour. She loves and thanks God because he is God, and therefore he is good. Only after this does she call God her Saviour, and this confession is a confession of faith, because she calls him her

Saviour before she sees convincing evidence of his salvation. He contrasts Mary's pure love with the impure love of those who do not praise God for his goodness, but only for his goodness to them. These people do not rejoice in their Saviour but only in their own salvation. They are fixated on the gift and neglect the Giver. They want God to do their will, but they refuse to do his will. The false gratitude of these people prevents God from giving them abundant gifts, above all the gift of salvation. Mary, however, is free. When she receives good things from God, she does not become attached to them; and when these good things are removed from her, she does not fall away from God. Whatever the circumstances, Mary has a grateful heart. She does not rejoice in the gifts, but in God. She 'clings only to God's goodness which she neither sees nor feels, overlooks the good things she does feel, and neither takes pleasure nor seeks her own enjoyment therein. Thus she can truly sing, "My spirit rejoices in God my Saviour"'.

'For he has looked upon the lowliness of his servant'. Luther remarks that Mary delights 'solely in the divine regard, which is so exceeding good and gracious that he deigned to look upon such a lowly maiden'. There is nothing trivial about 'the divine regard': the fact that God turns his face toward us means that we receive grace and salvation. Luther alludes to the psalms that invoke the radiance of God's face: Psalm 4 says 'lift up the light of your face upon us'; Psalm 67 pleads: 'May God be gracious and bless us, and make his face to shine upon us'. Luther emphasises that Mary does not glory in her virginity or in her humility but only in God's loving and gracious eyes that are turned toward her. He underlines the fact that Mary is truly humble and that 'true humility … never knows that it is humble'. This is the reason, he explains, why Mary is troubled at the veneration with which the angel Gabriel salutes her, since 'she had never expected the like'. She is happy in her lowliness and does not seek to be exalted or honoured. She does not become distracted by the great gifts that God has given her, nor does she boast of them, but instead goes beyond them to rise towards God, 'cling to him alone and highly esteem his goodness'. By contrast, those who have false humility are only content to speak and act humbly as long as the rich and mighty pay attention to them. But when people stop paying attention to them, they quickly abandon any pretence of lowliness: 'Men despise themselves, yet so as to be despised by no one else; they fly from honours, yet so as to be pursued by honours … But this holy Virgin points to naught else save her low estate. In it she was content to spend the remainder of her days, never seeking to be honoured or exalted, nor ever becoming aware of her own humility.'

'From this day forward all generations shall call me blessed'. Luther points out that Mary is clear about the reason she will be called blessed in the future: it is because God has turned his face towards her. 'Mary confesses that the foremost work God wrought for her was that he regarded her, which is indeed the greatest of his works, on which all the rest depend and from which they all derive. For where it comes to pass that God turns his face toward one to regard him, there is naught but grace and salvation, and all gifts and works must needs follow'. In other words, Mary attributes the source of her blessedness to God, and not to herself. She is not praising herself, but God. In Luther's view, Mary is 'the foremost example of the grace of God'. For this reason she is a model for us, encouraging us to trust in God's grace, to believe that he will look upon us graciously as well, and fill us with knowledge and love of him.

'For the Almighty has done great things for me, and holy is his name.' Luther equates 'the great things' with the stupendous truth 'that she became the Mother of God, in which work so many and such great good things are bestowed on her as pass man's understanding. For on this there follows all honour, all blessedness, and her unique place in the whole of mankind, among which she has no equal, namely, that she had a child by the Father in heaven, and such a child … Hence men have crowded all her glory into a single word, calling her the Mother of God. No one can say anything greater of her or to her, though he had as many tongues as there are leaves on the trees, or grass in the fields, or stars in the sky, or sand by the sea.'

Underlying this emphasis on Mary as the Mother of God is Luther's deep gratitude that God has taken on human flesh in the person of Jesus Christ. Who could have imagined that the transcendent Creator of the universe would have decided to enter our world as a weak and vulnerable child? Yet this is precisely what happened. On the one hand, God had to become a human being in order to suffer and die, but on the other hand he had to remain God for his death to become our forgiveness. It is because Jesus was born of the Virgin Mary that he is a true human being; it is because he is begotten of the Father from all eternity that he is true God. As Mother of God, no other creature is Mary's equal, because she had a child by the heavenly Father, and not just any child, but a divine child.

Luther stresses that Mary does not take any credit for giving birth to Jesus: 'For though she was without sin, yet that grace was too surpassing great for her to deserve it in any way. How should a creature deserve to become the Mother of God?' This is why, according to Luther, Mary adds the words, 'holy is his name': precisely to underscore that it is because of God's goodness. She recognises that it is all the work of God. Luther puts the following words onto the lips of Our Lady: 'None, therefore, should praise me or give me the glory for becoming the Mother of God, but God alone and his work are to be honoured and praised in me. It is enough to congratulate me and call me blessed, because God used me and wrought in me his works'.

It is becoming evident that the novelty of Luther's approach to Mary is that he focuses on what God achieves in her, and not on her own achievements. He highlights what God does in her, and not what she herself does. For Luther, Mary's response to God models what our response should be, because she opens herself completely to the mystery of God. The greatness of Mary is in her huge and grateful yes of faith, her surrender to God's loving plan for her. Luther places before our admiring gaze this self-effacing woman from Nazareth, who combines deep humility with complete trust in God. She is small enough and trusting enough to open herself to the unimaginable fullness of God's grace.

Luther highlights something crucial about Mary: she is not preoccupied with amassing merits, for the simple reason that she is not preoccupied with herself at all. She is not obsessed with doing as many good works as possible, as though she were lodging money in a spiritual bank to become her insurance policy on the Last Day. She simply gives and gives and gives, without attributing much importance to what she does, because her heart is fully focused on God. She doesn't want God to count up all her good works; instead, she pays constant attention to God's blessings so that she can give continual thanks to him. She does not seek to accomplish great deeds but instead to trust God completely and at every moment.

Luther emphasises that God's mercy reaches down to Mary on account of her littleness, precisely because she is poor in spirit. Divine love typically reaches down to those who are humble. 'O thou blessed Virgin, Mother of God, what great comfort hath God shown us in thee, by so graciously regarding thy unworthiness and low estate. Hereby we are encouraged to believe that he will henceforth not despise us poor and lowly ones, but graciously regard us also, according to thy example.'

In this same spirit, Luther is keen to underline how ordinary and everyday Mary is: 'To her neighbours and their daughters she was but a simple maiden, tending the cattle and doing the house-work, and doubtless esteemed no more than any poor maidservant today, who does as she is bidden about the house.' He contrasts Mary's humility with those who stand out from their fellow human beings through their prowess in prayer, fasting and good works, and so fall into the trap of pride. But sanctity cannot be equated with outward appearances or external works: 'There is no peace except where men teach that we are made pious, righteous and blessed by no work nor outward thing, but solely by faith, that is, a firm confidence in the unseen grace of God that is promised to us.' Luther is adamant that God came into our world in order to save human beings within the world, and not to encourage them to adopt sanctimonious airs and graces. He describes this kind of dangerous pride in the following way: 'Every one strives after that which is above him, after honour, power, wealth, knowledge, a life of ease, and whatever is lofty and great. And where such folk are, there are many hangers-on, all the world gathers round them, gladly yields them service, and would be by their side and share their high estate.' They equate salvation with upward mobility, whether in terms of money, power, comfort or knowledge. Luther notes by contrast that Mary is so nondescript that the daughter of the high priest Caiaphas would not have even have deigned to employ her as a maid, and he concludes: 'Thus God's work and his eyes are in the depths, but man's only in the height.'

At this point the first part of the Magnificat comes to an end. Having thanked God for everything he has done for her, Mary now moves on in the second part of the Magnificat to celebrate God's goodness toward humanity in general. In doing this, Mary shows us how to recognise God's gifts and how to express our gratitude for them. She lists six divine works, beginning with the noblest of all, God's mercy: 'and his mercy is from age to age on those who fear him'. Luther says that those who fear God are the poor in spirit; in other words those who are aware of their dependence upon God, and who recognise that everything they have is a gift from God. 'This, then, is the first work of God – that he is merciful to all who are … willing to be poor in spirit … who truly fear God, who count themselves not worthy of anything … who ascribe whatever they have to his pure grace'. To be poor in spirit is quite a challenge: it means to be willing to stop clinging even to spiritual experiences if they deflect us from God. For instance, people with the gift of healing can become so excited by the fact that they possess this gift that they can stop exercising it for the benefit of others and instead do it in order to win plaudits for themselves.

The second divine work is to scatter the proud-hearted. The proud of heart imagine that it is their power that links them to God, whereas it is in fact the honest admission of neediness that draws God towards us. When people exalt themselves, God 'withdraws his power from them and lets them puff themselves up in their own power alone. For where man's strength begins, God's strength ends.' Although he firmly criticises the rich and the powerful, Luther reserves his strongest censure for those who take pride in their own wisdom: 'The rich destroy the truth among themselves; the mighty drive it away from others; but these wise ones utterly extinguish the truth itself.'

The third divine work is casting the mighty from their thrones. Luther remarks that the fall of great empires such as Babylon or Rome is evidence that God sooner or later takes away power if it is not used for good purposes.

The fourth divine work is raising the lowly. Luther makes it clear that raising the lowly does not mean putting them on the seats from which the powerful have been dethroned. If that were to happen, they could very well end up replicating the proud conduct of the mighty. Instead, it is a matter of exalting the lowly in a spiritual way, an exaltation that may have to wait until the Day of Judgement, but which will nonetheless arrive.

The fifth and sixth works are filling the hungry with good things and sending the rich away empty. Luther notes that 'by the hungry are not meant those who have little or nothing to eat, but those who gladly suffer want, especially if they are forcibly compelled by others to do so for God's sake or the truth'. Suffering want is an invitation to put our trust in God, so that what we do is God's work; just as being lowly or bereft of human help is an invitation to rely on God to do the work.

After singing her praises of God's work in her own life and in the life of humanity at large, Mary concludes the Magnificat by saying, 'he protects Israel, his servant, remembering his mercy'. In these words of Mary's canticle, Luther recognises an allusion to the greatest divine work of all – the incarnation, where God becomes one of us.

And so we arrive at the final phrase of the Magnificat: 'the mercy promised to our fathers, to Abraham and his sons for ever'. Luther emphasises that God does not help Israel in reward for anything Israel has achieved, but because of his promise. God has made this promise out of pure love, and because of this same love he fulfils his promise.

Luther clearly treasures this prayer of Mary. Already in the prologue to his commentary, he praises the daily custom of singing the Magnificat as part of evening prayer in all churches, and he adds that it should be sung in a way 'that distinguishes it from the other chants'. Not only has Luther a soft spot for the Magnificat, he also has a soft spot for the Mother of God, whom he again and again describes as 'tender' or 'sweet'. This fondness is shown by the fact that although Luther is against asking the saints to intercede for us, he makes an exception in the case of Mary. Both at the beginning and at the end of his commentary on the Magnificat, he turns to Mary. In the prologue he writes: 'May the tender Mother of God herself procure for me the spirit of wisdom, profitably and thoroughly to expound this song of hers.' And as he ends his commentary, Luther writes in a similar vein: 'We pray God to give us a right understanding of this Magnificat, an understanding that consists not merely in brilliant words, but glowing life in body and soul. May Christ grant this through the intercession and for the sake of his dear Mother Mary.' Presumably Luther feels even more comfortable with the prospect of calling upon Mary's intercession because there is a biblical foundation for it. In the story of the Wedding at Cana in Saint John's Gospel, it is Mary who intercedes with Jesus on behalf of the wedding guests.

Apart from the helpful reflections upon gratitude to be gleaned from Luther's commentary on the Magnificat, Catholics can learn another crucial lesson from it: the truth that Mary is the outstanding example of God's mercy and grace in action. God chooses the lowly, not because of any merit of their own, but on account of his infinite love: 'This, therefore, is what Mary means: "God hath regarded me, a poor, despised and lowly maiden, though he might have found a rich, renowned, noble and mighty queen, the daughter of princes and great lords. He might have found the daughter of Annas or of Caiaphas, who were the first folk in the land. But he let his pure and gracious eyes light on me, and used so poor and despised a maiden, in order that no one might glory in his presence, as though he were worthy of this, and that I must needs acknowledge all to be pure grace and goodness and no whit my merit or worthiness."' The gratuitous nature of God's love is reflected in a small way in the love a father or mother has for a little child. The child isn't loved because of anything it has merited or deserved. Instead, without the prompting of the child, without the child even asking for love, the father and mother freely bestow their love upon it.

Interestingly, the Immaculate Conception reinforces the point that Luther is making. For the Immaculate Conception – the teaching that Mary was filled with grace from the first moment of her conception – is not something that Mary could have ever deserved or merited, since there was no Mary there before the gift was given. She received this astonishing gift at the same moment that she received the gift of life itself. This gift was all God's initiative. From the first moment of her conception, God chose to make Mary into the stand-out example of his mercy. Her being was filled to overflowing with God's merciful love, as the angel Gabriel makes clear at the Annunciation, when he hails her as 'filled with grace'.

In later years, Luther became more wary of giving too much honour to Mary, since he was concerned that this might compromise the honour owed to God. Nevertheless, he did not lose his regard for Mary. Let's finish this section with a couple of quotations from later sermons of Martin Luther. They testify to his enduring affection for the Virgin Mary.

> It is the consolation and the superabundant goodness of God, that humanity is able to exult in such a treasure. Mary is its true Mother. (Sermon of Christmas, 1529)

> She is nobility, wisdom, and holiness personified. We can never honour her enough. Still, honour and praise must be given to her in such a way as to hurt neither Christ nor the scriptures. (Sermon of Christmas, 1531)

Mary in Søren Kierkegaard's Writings

Philosophers aren't always complimentary about their peers. Arthur Schopenhauer, for instance, who lectured at the University of Berlin at the same time as Georg Friedrich Wilhelm Hegel, was highly critical of his more famous colleague. So much so that, a number of years later, Schopenhauer pronounced the following judgement on Hegel's philosophy: 'But the height of audacity in serving up pure nonsense, in stringing together senseless and extravagant mazes of words, such as had previously been known only in madhouses, was finally reached in Hegel, and became the instrument of the most barefaced general mystification that has ever taken place, with a result which will appear fabulous to posterity, and will remain as a monument to German stupidity.' For that reason it is even more striking when one philosopher expresses admiration for another. Ludwig Wittgenstein, arguably one of the greatest philosophers of the twentieth century, was effusive in his praise of the Danish philosopher, Søren Kierkegaard. Wittgenstein put it this way: 'Kierkegaard was by far the most profound thinker of the last century. Kierkegaard was a saint.'

Kierkegaard's perspective on Mary points to her as a strong woman, and not a weak wimp. Additionally, he shows how she can help us take faith more seriously, while treating anxiety less seriously. (Here I'm not referring to the kind of anxiety disorder that needs professional help, but to the inevitable anxiety of everyday life.)

Kierkegaard was dismayed that faith had become watered down in the Danish society of his era. He was brought up in a devout Lutheran household, and valued the traditional Lutheran emphasis upon faith as an inner and personal relationship with God. But he became increasingly critical of the established Church of Denmark, because it seemed content with mere external observance. He was drawn to the figure of Mary because he could see clearly that her faith was so much more than lip service. Correspondingly, Kierkegaard's own admiration for Mary was much more than skin-deep; it was true and heartfelt. Whenever he mentions Mary in his journals, he describes her as pure, faithful, full of grace, or in similarly positive terms.

One of his most well-known works, *Fear and Trembling*, includes a thought-provoking reflection upon the greatness of Mary's faith. Kierkegaard published *Fear and Trembling* under a fictional name, Johannes de Silentio (John of Silence), to show that it is hard to speak about faith in an adequate way. Faith is so mysterious that it often reduces us to a perplexed or even hushed silence. To show how difficult true faith is, *Fear and Trembling* focuses on a traumatic event in the life of the biblical figure Abraham, the moment when God tested his faith by commanding him to sacrifice his son Isaac on Mount Moriah.

Although we applaud Abraham for what he has done, John of Silence notes that it's easy to forget the consuming background toil that it takes to be a hero. As a contemporary example, we could reflect upon a tennis player winning Wimbledon with seemingly effortless elegance. It all looks so easy, and so we forget the long investment of blood, sweat and tears that makes such a victory possible. We don't call to mind the years of relentless training, the sacrifice of so many other activities, and the dogged persistence in the face of setbacks and failures.

John of Silence sees a similar forgetfulness afflicting our admiration of Mary. We speak glibly of her greatness, but that is because we know how the story finally turned out: Jesus rose from the dead and Christianity took root, spreading right across the world. Moreover, we actually deceive ourselves by focusing only on the result, conveniently forgetting the costly road that led to her greatness.

We're so familiar with Mary's story that we imagine we can easily make sense of it. But sometimes we are blind to the true magnitude of what is right before our eyes. The Greek philosopher Aristotle remarks in his *Metaphysics*: 'Our eyes are like those of the owl. As the eyes of the owl are blinded by the brightness of daylight, so the intelligence of our soul is blind to what in itself is most evident.'

John of Silence praises Mary with these words: 'Was there ever in the world anyone as great as that blessed woman, the mother of God, the Virgin Mary? And yet how do people speak of her? To say she was favoured among women doesn't make her great ... What is left out is the distress, the anxiety, the paradox ... No doubt Mary bore the child miraculously, but ... such a time is one of anxiety, distress, and paradox. No doubt the angel was a ministering spirit, but he was not an obliging one who went round to all the other young girls in Israel and said: "Do not despise Mary, something out of the ordinary is happening to her". The angel came only to Mary, and no one could understand her.'

Kierkegaard, through his mouthpiece John of Silence, is here calling attention to Mary's faith. The angel Gabriel effectively asks Mary to abandon the future she has mapped out for herself. She has never contemplated becoming a mother or having a child, since she is fully given to God. Now she is being asked to change all that. This is already a leap of faith: to have enough confidence to be willing to let go of her own project so that she can embrace God's mysterious plan. But that's not all, not by any means. She is also being asked to believe something that is humanly impossible: she is told that she will conceive even though there will be no man in the picture. This is not how conception happens, and Mary knows it: women simply don't conceive without a man's involvement. To believe that it would happen in any other way is to be asked to believe the impossible. And why should this kind of impossibility be promised to her, of all people? To someone who has already excluded herself from motherhood, an exclusion, moreover, with which God himself seems to be well pleased? After all that has gone beforehand, after everything that has made such sense in her life, it appears nonsensical that all of a sudden she should be called to be the Mother of God. There are too many unanswered questions for her to be able to make sense of it all. It is not even clear how the angel in front of her fits into this strange pantomime. Is she about to wake up from a crazy dream or, worse still, an absurd nightmare?

And yet the extraordinary thing is that although Mary doesn't understand, she believes. In *Concluding Unscientific Postscript*, Kierkegaard writes (again, through the voice of a pseudonym): 'If I wish to preserve myself in faith I must constantly be intent upon holding fast the objective uncertainty, so as to remain out upon the deep, over seventy thousand fathoms of water, still preserving my faith.' Mary held fast to 'the objective uncertainty' in the sense that she did not ask the angel for evidence or proof. She was ready to remain floating over that vastly deep ocean with no visible anchor nearby and no shoreline in sight. Seventy thousand fathoms is no joke: it's the equivalent of eighty miles or 130 kilometres.

If you are floating on the ocean with eighty miles of water beneath you, thrashing about in panic is a recipe for disaster – it is only going to make you sink more quickly. If you start focusing on yourself and your precarious position, you're likely to start by worrying and end by panicking. However, if you manage to trust enough to relax, you will be able to float. Mary trusted God, and so, despite the water beneath her descending to an unimaginable depth, she stayed afloat, not because of herself, but on account of God's all-powerful buoyancy.

Mary's gift of herself to God was incredibly courageous, for it also included an intuition about future suffering that would break most people. The rest of us are blessed with not knowing what lies ahead. Even though we're curious about the future, our ignorance of it in fact frees us from a weight that we are too fragile to carry. But the future must have been unveiled to some extent for Mary. After all, she would have been familiar with the prophecies of the suffering servant from Isaiah; she clearly heard Simeon's sombre words when she presented the child Jesus in the Temple: 'and a sword shall pierce your own soul'. When you can see huge pain clearly looming on the horizon, suffering puts down deep roots in your soul and stays stubbornly entrenched.

And so, in *Fear and Trembling*, John of Silence rejects the prettified picture of Mary sitting vacuously in a sumptuous setting and mindlessly engaging with the child Jesus. He comments: 'She is not at all the fine lady sitting in her finery and playing with a divine child'. Her courage was unparalleled. Here is a woman who accepted the intimidating invitation to become the mother of God's only-begotten Son without knowing how this pregnancy would affect her reputation and social standing. She became pregnant before she and Joseph came to live under the same roof. Sooner or later, Joseph would realise she was with child, and he would know that the child was not his. Would her fiancé be willing to stand by her if his own reputation were to become tarnished in the eyes of the world? Would he be able to endure the scornful remarks and disparaging glances? And if he didn't stand by her, would she be stoned to death under Jewish law? 'If … no proof of the young woman's virginity can be found, she shall be brought to the door of her father's house and there the men of her town shall stone her to death' (Deut 22:20–21). Despite these terrifying prospects, Mary had the strength to say, 'Be it done unto me according to thy word'.

Just as Abraham is greater than any hero, so Mary is greater than any heroine. Returning to our Wimbledon example, we can understand to some extent the sacrifice that is demanded to become a tennis champion: this kind of heroism makes sense. However, we cannot understand Mary's greatness, because it is inner, and this corresponds to Kierkegaard's vision of faith as an inward, personal commitment that is invisible to the outside observer. The angel Gabriel didn't explain to the other women of Galilee what had happened to Mary. Neither did he explain it to Joseph. And who would have believed Mary if she herself had told them that she was with child through the overshadowing of the Holy Spirit?

Moreover, Mary's day-to-day behaviour did not reveal heroic traits; she did not show any signs of being out of the ordinary. She visited her cousin Elizabeth, gave birth to Jesus in simple surroundings in Bethlehem and, after returning from Egypt, reared him in the nondescript town of Nazareth. It would have been impossible to mark her out from other people. There was nothing external to set her apart: no spectacular signs and no noteworthy happenings. And yet within the silence of that commonplace life, something wonderful was unfolding. Mary's silence was opening up a vast space for God to be heard.

Kierkegaard was keenly aware of the revelatory power of silence. He knew that its very uselessness was more useful than so many apparently useful things. In *For Self-Examination* he writes: 'in observing the present state of the world and life in general, from a Christian point of view one has to say: it is a disease. And if I were a physician and someone asked me, "What do you think should be done?" I would answer, "the first thing … the very first thing that must be done is: create silence, bring about silence. God's Word cannot be heard, and if in order to be heard in the hullabaloo it must be shouted deafeningly with noisy instruments, then it is not God's Word; create silence!"'

In *The Present Age*, Kierkegaard laments that all our attention is directed outwards: 'people's attention is no longer turned inwards'. He remarks (prophetically) that 'ours is the world of advertisement and publicity'. Even though he died in 1855, he was already attuned to the distracting nature of the media, and saddened by the affliction of what he called 'talkativeness'. He knew that there was a need to dig beneath the surface clatter of talkativeness to find the silence that enveloped Mary, the silence that enables us to hear the loving voice of God and respond to it.

Mary's silence was not only the patient sense of expectation that filled her during her pregnancy; it was also a deep silence that pervaded her entire life as she bravely confided in God, trusting that he would lead her. Her silence was not merely the absence of words; it was very much the fullness of listening, a continual listening to the word of God, a listening that embraced both joy and sorrow. As Kierkegaard puts it in *Without Authority*: 'From a woman you learn the quiet, deep, godly sorrow that is silent before God, from Mary'.

Within Mary's heart, invisible to the eye, there was a deep passion for God. Passion is a word that Kierkegaard associates with faith. When we hear the word 'faith', it often brings to mind something theoretical, such as a proposition or concept. But this is precisely what Kierkegaard does *not* mean by faith. For Kierkegaard, faith is above all passion, because unless faith is about a God who loves us and reaches out to tell us this, it is useless. Passion is something he found conspicuously lacking in his era. *The Present Age* begins with the following arresting sentence: 'Our age is essentially one of understanding and reflection, without passion, momentarily bursting into enthusiasm, and shrewdly relapsing into repose.'

Our English word 'passion' has its roots in the Latin word for suffering. And for Kierkegaard passion involves a struggle: to believe in something that other people easily dismiss as foolishness. Mary had this passion, and because of it she was willing to commit the apparent foolishness of believing the words of the angel Gabriel. That an unknown teenager from a forgotten town in Galilee was to become the mother of God was something that could not be rationally explained, a flight of fancy too outrageous for anyone even to entertain.

The great heroes of faith have a heroism beyond our noblest ideals of the heroic. There is no language to express their nobility. In *Fear and Trembling* Kierkegaard says of Mary and Abraham: 'She needs no worldly admiration, as little as Abraham needs our tears, for she was no heroine and he no hero, but both of them became greater than that, not by any means by being relieved of the distress, the agony, and the paradox, but because of these.'

We need the example of someone like Mary to reawaken the true passion of our faith, because otherwise we are in danger of sinking into the kind of mediocrity that Kierkegaard rightly castigated. In his journals, he gives vent to his frustration with half-heartedness: 'The greatest danger to Christianity is, I contend, not heresies, heterodoxies, not atheists, not profane secularism – no, but the kind of orthodoxy which is cordial drivel, hearty twaddle, mediocrity with a dash of sugar … perpetually polite, so small, so nice … but the very essence of Christianity is utterly opposed to this mediocrity.'

Mary was anything but mediocre. She was so in touch with the invisible that she could believe the impossible. At the time of the Annunciation, the angel Gabriel reassured her that 'nothing is impossible for God'. Kierkegaard was intrigued by the link between God and possibility, a connection he refers to at several points in his writings. He was convinced that believing in God opened up a world of infinite possibilities. It was this God of the impossible who liberated Mary. Yet her freedom did not exempt her from anxiety.

The main point Kierkegaard makes about anxiety is that it isn't something to be avoided, but a force to be wrestled with in order to arrive at a more authentic way of living. He describes anxiety as 'the dizziness of freedom'. It is a fitting image. When we're dizzy, things spin round and appear distorted. And because of this, we ourselves lack balance and can't find our centre. The temptation is to relieve the sense of dizziness as quickly as possible by clinging to whatever foothold we can find. But if, instead, we can stay with the dizziness, and be patient with the gap it opens up in our secure stance in the world, we can find a new freedom. Anxiety then turns out to be, not so much an obstacle to freedom, but an opening into the whole world of possibility.

Mary experienced anxiety on many occasions. She became pregnant – and Joseph didn't understand. Later, when her pregnancy was advanced, she made the long and uncomfortable journey to Bethlehem on a donkey. When Joseph and she arrived there, they could not find a suitable place for her to give birth to Jesus. In the Temple, Simeon told her that a sword would pierce her heart. She and Joseph had to get up in the middle of the night and flee to Egypt because Herod was out to kill Jesus. After their return, when Jesus was twelve years old, she lost him for three days. When Jesus began his public ministry, she suffered when he encountered opposition, criticism, mockery and scorn. At the time of his passion, she underwent anguish when one of the twelve betrayed him. She suffering quietly at the Cross as Jesus was subjected to a slow and torturous death. And she struggled with everything in her to keep believing until his resurrection.

Yet despite all the anxiety, she was never overwhelmed. Kierkegaard admired Mary's huge confidence, quiet courage, and extraordinary resilience. Her confidence was so immense that she always believed God was on her side – and even at her side. She lived constantly in his presence, and surrendered herself to him in every circumstance. Despite the many sorrows she endured, she knew that nothing happened by chance. She did not see the value of every trial at the moment it occurred, yet she was certain that with the benefit of hindsight she would recognise God's mercy at work in every one of them.

Her courage was gentle because it was not a matter of physical strength, the kind of brute force that intimidates others. But neither was it a matter of the kind of strength that imposes its own ideas on others. In fact, her courage was not about putting herself above others in any way. It was based instead on putting God above herself, and on placing her trust in him, which meant that instead of viewing courage as always holding on to things, Mary realised that it was often about letting go. Kierkegaard is fond of quoting her reply to the invitation to become the mother of Jesus, a reply where Mary lets go: 'Be it done unto me according to thy word.'

Mary was not only hugely confident and gently courageous; she was also enormously resilient. If a piece of metal is resilient, it can regain its original shape after being twisted or stretched. Despite being put under pressure, it is able to return to its initial form. It has the elasticity to cope with stress. At other times, the effect of stretching strengthens it, so that the next time it is flexed it resists deformation in an even more robust way. In *Without Authority* Kierkegaard remarks: 'It indeed happened, as was prophesied, that a sword did pierce her heart, but she did not despair – either over the prophecy or when it was fulfilled.' Mary's resilience was strengthened because the words of Simeon – a sword will pierce your heart – gave her the opportunity to prepare beforehand. She already knew that becoming the mother of Jesus would turn her life upside down. Simeon's words gave her an indication of just how painful this upheaval would be. We say 'forewarned is forearmed', and the dangers we anticipate strike us with less intensity. When trials take us by complete surprise, the flood of fear can be overwhelming. But if we prepare ourselves for the possibility of trials, we are less likely to be overcome by fear, and more likely to face them with some level of composure and courage.

Mary, of course, was especially helped by the simplicity of her spirit. She looked upon everything that happened as God's gift to her. In a sense, she saw through every event to see God in it. The actual nature of her duty at any given moment didn't distract her from giving her attention to God. In our case, we become easily distracted by the sheer abundance of stimuli that bombard us each day. But we are also canny enough to know we're missing out: surface living leaves us really empty. Kierkegaard conveys this in a chilling sentence: 'I have just now come from a party where I was its life and soul; witticisms streamed from my lips, everyone laughed and admired me, but I went away – yes, the dash should be as long as the radius of the earth's orbit – and wanted to shoot myself.'

As for Mary, Kierkegaard notes in *Concluding Unscientific Postscript* that once she received the message of the angel Gabriel, she 'concealed the words as a treasure in the beautiful setting of a good heart'. Mary cherished these words because she fully trusted God. And because of this immense trust, she was certain that everything would work out for the good. She knew that God would not test her beyond her strength. Nevertheless, she was familiar with the wisdom expressed by the Book of Sirach: 'My child, when you come to serve the Lord, prepare yourself for trials'. Kierkegaard regards Abraham as our father in faith, because he was ready to sacrifice his son Isaac, a sacrifice from which he was spared at the last moment. But he identifies Mary's faith as even more radical, because her son Jesus was really sacrificed. She is our mother in faith.

Kierkegaard is acutely conscious of the virtue at the foundation of Mary's life: her humility. She saw herself as God's handmaid, and did not presume to start something until God gave her the grace to begin it. She knew that otherwise she might be tempted to do things for her own glory, and not for the glory of God. She was happy to live completely dependent upon God, fully trusting his fidelity and his promises, and so discerning his loving design in all that happened in her life. In these simple yet dignified words from Kierkegaard's *The Book of Adler*: 'She remained the same quiet, humble woman ... she believed.'

Dietrich Bonhoeffer's Advent Sermon of 1933

'This song of Mary's is the oldest Advent hymn. It is the most passionate, most vehement, one might almost say, most revolutionary Advent hymn ever sung. It is not the gentle, sweet, dreamy Mary that we so often see portrayed in pictures, but the passionate, powerful, proud, enthusiastic Mary, who speaks here.'

With these burning and urgent words, Dietrich Bonhoeffer began a sermon on the Magnificat on the third Sunday of Advent in 1933. This Lutheran pastor and theologian was preaching at the end of the first year of the Nazi dictatorship in Germany. Although the sermon was delivered in London, it was given in German to a German-speaking congregation, and the parallels with the situation in Bonhoeffer's home country were unmistakable and fully intended.

Despite dying at the relatively young age of thirty-nine, Dietrich Bonhoeffer has caught the imagination of Christians worldwide, not only because of his originality as a theologian, but most of all because he was one of the few pastors or priests to resist the Nazi dictatorship in a courageous and consistent way. Because of his alleged links to several plots to assassinate Adolf Hitler (allegations that were never proven), Bonhoeffer was executed by hanging in Flossenbürg concentration camp on 9 April, 1945.

Bonhoeffer's readiness to translate his thoughts into action is what continues to draw so many people to him, aware as they are that so often terrible injustices are perpetuated because too many people are afraid to do precisely what Bonhoeffer did. In the words of Bonhoeffer's friend and fellow Lutheran pastor, Martin Niemöller: 'First they came for the socialists, and I did not speak out – because I was not a socialist. Then they came for the trade unionists, and I did not speak out – because I was not a trade unionist. Then they came for the Jews, and I did not speak out – because I was not a Jew. Then they came for me – and there was no one left to speak for me.'

Bonhoeffer was an avid admirer of Kierkegaard, whom he regarded as a genuine Christian thinker, alongside Saint Paul, Saint Augustine, Martin Luther, and the twentieth-century Swiss theologian Karl Barth. It was Kierkegaard who inspired Bonhoeffer to read the Bible like a love letter, with the confident expectation that it was communicating a heartfelt and profound message. Bonhoeffer heartened to Kierkegaard's insistence on how our decisions and choices shape us.

In his monumental and authoritative biography on Bonhoeffer, his student and friend Eberhard Bethge calls Bonhoeffer's 1939 choice to return to Germany, 'the great decision of his life'. This is undoubtedly true, and because it was such a significant decision, it was also a major turning point. But another milestone in Bonhoeffer's short but dramatic life took shape several years beforehand. It was a turning point that began at the end of the 1920s, and received its definitive seal in 1933, a year that proved to be decisive for the entire German nation. And it was towards the end of that same year of 1933 that Bonhoeffer preached his extraordinary sermon on Our Lady's Magnificat.

Bonhoeffer wrote about this turning point in a letter of 1 January 1936 to Elizabeth Zinn, a former girlfriend of his. 'Then something happened, something that has changed and transformed my life to the present day. For the first time I discovered the Bible … I had often preached. I had seen a great deal of the Church, and talked and preached about it – but I had not yet become a Christian … I know that at that time I turned the doctrine of Christ into something of personal advantage for myself … Also I had never prayed, or prayed only very little. For all my loneliness, I was quite pleased with myself. Then the Bible, and in particular the Sermon on the Mount, freed me from that. Since then everything has changed. I have felt this plainly, and so have other people about me … Then came the crisis of 1933. This strengthened me in it. Also I now found others who shared this aim with me.'

What factors helped Bonhoeffer come to the point where he could say that 'everything has changed'? In terms of immediate influences, he mentions four crucial factors in this letter: reading the Bible, particularly the Sermon on the Mount; praying; the reinforcement he found through 'the crisis of 1933'; and the discovery of kindred spirits.

There was also the experience of working as a curate for a German-speaking congregation in Barcelona, from 1928 to 1929. Walking around the city, Bonhoeffer was struck by the poverty he saw. In a letter to a friend he wrote: 'Here one meets people as they are, away from the masquerade of the "Christian world," people with passions, criminal types, little people with little ambitions, little desires, and little sins, all in all people who feel homeless in both senses of the word, who loosen up if one talks to them in a friendly way, real people.'

On returning to Germany he completed his post-doctoral qualification at the University of Berlin. In 1930 he travelled to New York, where he studied at Union Theological Seminary. However, the most significant part of his education that year occurred outside the classroom. Each Sunday he went to the Abyssinian Baptist Church in Harlem, taught Sunday school classes, helped out in the church's youth clubs, and fell in love with black Gospel music. The New York experience woke him up to the reality of racism and to the important link between religion and justice. After his year in New York, Bonhoeffer returned to Berlin in 1931, and began lecturing in theology. In Berlin he once again reached out to the marginalised, spending several months living and working in one of the poorest slums of the city.

So, on 30 January 1933, when Adolph Hitler was appointed Chancellor of the German Reich, Bonhoeffer was spiritually ready to respond. By then he was praying regularly, reading the Bible, and especially the Sermon on the Mount. Indeed, he would later write to Mahatma Gandhi, himself a great admirer of that famous sermon of Jesus, with the intention – which he never realised – of going to India to live in Gandhi's presence and absorb his teaching. To cap it all, Bonhoeffer had learned from the poor of Barcelona, Harlem and Berlin.

Two days after Hitler became chancellor, on 1 February 1933, the twenty-six-year-old Bonhoeffer gave an address on national radio called 'The Younger Generation's Changed View of the Concept of Führer'. His words were forceful: 'Should the leader allow himself to succumb to the wishes of those he leads, who will always seek to turn him into an idol, then the image of the leader will gradually become the image of the seducer. This is the leader who makes an idol of himself and his office and who thus mocks God.'

Bonhoeffer made use of an interesting play on words during this radio broadcast. The German word for 'leader' is *Führer*, while the word for 'seducer' sounds quite similar: *Verführer*. According to Bonhoeffer, not only were the two words really close (with a difference of only three letters between them), but also the reality was too close for comfort: a leader could easily degenerate into a seducer. We know that the Nazi regime was tuned in to the national radio channel that day, because Bonhoeffer's radio address was abruptly cut off while he was still in mid-sentence. But this wasn't enough to stop Bonhoeffer. Two months later, in April 1933, he wrote an essay called 'The Church and the Jewish Question' in response to the boycott of Jewish stores and business, and the exclusion of Jews from the civil service, all of which happened in the first week of April 1933.

Bonhoeffer was one of the few theologians brave enough to show solidarity with the Jewish population of Germany. Faced with the deplorable treatment of German Jewish citizens, he called upon the churches to do something to help all Jews. In effect, he was urging them to stand up to the Nazi regime in the process. Church leaders failed to take up his challenge.

In August 1933, Bonhoeffer and others put together a landmark church document which showed the first signs of a welcome change in Christian attitudes toward Jewish people. The 'Bethel Confession' was in response to the new laws and boycotts against the Jews in Nazi Germany. The document included a forceful denunciation of Nazi-led anti-Semitism. It appealed to Christians to stand up for the Jews instead of deserting them.

It is clear, then, that 1933 was a turning point in Bonhoeffer's life. Born into privilege, he had the intellect, self-confidence and family connections to chart out a secure and protected career for himself as a professor and pastor. But instead of sitting at his writing desk or standing at the pulpit, he gave the kind of witness that went well beyond writing and lecturing.

In the autumn of 1933 he left Germany for England. His resistance to the Nazis was not in doubt, but perhaps he hoped that the change of scene would give him the opportunity to figure out how to develop his opposition in the future. However, in England he found himself both too near and too far from Germany. Only a few months after arriving in London, he wrote to one of his brothers: 'Here you find yourself too close at hand not to want to take part in everything and yet too far away really to join actively in anything'. The year and a half in London was to be the only time in his life that he worked as a full-time pastor. He lived in a vicarage in the south London suburb of Forest Hill. It was draughty, damp and infested with mice, but none of this dampened Bonhoeffer's spirits. He became pastor to two small German-speaking parishes in London. His predecessor had preached easy-going and pious sermons. By comparison, the parishioners found their new pastor's style much too challenging and uncompromising. Bonhoeffer prepared his sermons thoroughly, writing them out word for word, often sending the manuscripts back to friends in Germany. As a result, sixteen of his London sermons have been preserved.

On 17 December 1933, the third Sunday of Advent, he gave his stirring sermon on the Magnificat. Bonhoeffer effectively warned his congregation against domesticating the innate wildness of the Magnificat. There is a lesson here for Catholics too. We can become so familiar with Mary's song that the words lose their prophetic edge. We can dilute the radical parts with so much sugar that they lose their acerbic quality altogether. Perhaps we sentimentalise the Magnificat because we don't know how to deal with its uncomfortable phrases. But that is to betray the reality of this song, which proclaims God's preferential love for the poor and the lowly.

Mary sings her song in the house of Zechariah, although there is no sign of Zechariah himself. It is two women who take centre stage; no male voice is to be heard. In any case, Zechariah isn't in a position to speak. When the angel told him his wife Elizabeth was to conceive in her old age, he couldn't believe it and asked for proof. He received a kind of proof he didn't expect – he was struck dumb until everything the angel had promised should come to pass.

It is difficult to summarise Bonhoeffer's sermon, and not just because of the content. There is also a particular tone to it. You would have had to be there in person to catch the impassioned tone in which he delivered it. Given the limits of the printed word, I'll nevertheless try to be as faithful as possible to both his content and tone. He begins by calling the Magnificat 'the oldest Advent hymn'. He stresses how different it is from sentimental Christmas carols. It is a hymn that is sung with enthusiasm, fervour and passion, because it is a song about bringing down the mighty and humbling the proud, about the power of God compared to the powerlessness of human beings. It echoes the sentiments of far-sighted women from the Old Testament such as Deborah, Judith and Miriam.

Bonhoeffer describes how Mary is full of the Holy Spirit, ready to do what God asks of her, and she now speaks through her Magnificat about the huge event of God's coming into the world. She knows in her own body the truth of the amazing things that God does. She knows that God's ways are far above our ways.

Indeed, God is liable to be found precisely where our reason is offended, where our piety is shaken out of its complacency, and where we find ourselves taking umbrage. God destroys the wisdom of those who claim to be wise, so that it is only the humble who can trust him and rejoice in his surprising ways. And God's goal is to raise up the lowly. 'That is the wonder of wonders, that God loves the lowly.' God chooses Mary precisely because she is lowly and insignificant. He chooses her in order to make her great. As Bonhoeffer puts it, God 'loves the lost ... where men say "lost", he says "found"; where men say "no", he says "yes".'

Bonhoeffer emphasises that God's choice of Mary and his decision to come into our world 'was no romantic family portrait, but the beginning of a total turning point, a new ordering of all things on this earth'. If we want to become part of this new order, we cannot be mere spectators; we must enter into the drama. We cannot approach the manger in a casual manner, because the one who is born there is both judge and Saviour of the world. When we enter the manger, we'll find ourselves either condemned or delivered, we will either 'be broken in pieces or know the compassion of God'. Encountering the Christ child is not child's play, because he is the one who dethrones sovereigns and brings down the proud.

Bonhoeffer remarks that there are two places that make the mighty and powerful of this world tremble: the manger in Bethlehem and the cross on Calvary. Even Herod didn't come near the manger. 'Before the Virgin Mary, before the manger of Christ, before God in his lowly state, the rich have no rights and no hope. They are convicted.' Proud people may imagine that they are safe, but sooner or later God will cast them down from their thrones and raise up the humble: 'For this purpose, Jesus Christ as the child in the manger, as the son of Mary, has come into the world.'

The manger forces us to decide what we count as important and unimportant in human life. Not everyone is powerful, but even many of those with little power are intent on exercising what power they have and dream only of expanding their power. But God doesn't think like that. God wants to lower himself, and it is only in lowliness that we will meet him.

To celebrate Christmas properly we must lay down at the manger all our power, pride and selfishness. Bonhoeffer concludes: 'Who is content to be lowly and to let God alone be high? Who sees the glory of God in the humble state of the child in the manger? Who says with Mary: "The Lord has been mindful of my humble state. My soul praises the Lord and my spirit rejoices in God my Saviour"? Amen.'

Bonhoeffer himself became poor and lowly like Mary. He lay down his power and privilege at the manger, and later, when he was executed, at the cross. And he had a mountain of privilege to cast aside. He was born into a family with impeccable social credentials. His father was a professor of psychology and neurology. His mother's father was a pastor, professor of theology and for a time the chaplain to the final German emperor, Kaiser Wilhelm II. If you've ever read Thomas Mann's first novel, *Buddenbrooks*, it gives you some sense of what it must have been like for Dietrich Bonhoeffer to have been born into a family with such a distinguished history behind it, and such a strong sense of destiny undergirding it.

To pursue his principles, he was ready to court the criticism, if not contempt, of friends, colleagues and the conformist society around him. His legacy in some ways echoes that of Mary. He was imprisoned, and she stood at the cross. Bonhoeffer inspires us not so much on account of his words or writings, but because he lived in the certainty that God was real, and in the sure knowledge that God's reality not only gave him strength and consolation but also imposed on him the obligation to reach out to the lowly and to stand up for what was right.

Like Mary, Bonhoeffer was able to see light in the darkness, and hope where others saw only despair. Ten years after his Advent sermon on the Magnificat, he wrote an Advent letter from prison to his fiancée, Maria von Wedemeyer, on 13 December 1943: 'And then, just when everything is bearing down on us to such an extent that we can scarcely withstand it, the Christmas message comes to tell us that all our ideas are wrong, and that what we take to be evil and dark is really good and light because it comes from God. Our eyes are at fault, that is all. God is in the manger, wealth in poverty, light in darkness, succour in abandonment. No evil can befall us; whatever men may do to us, they cannot but serve the God who is secretly revealed as love and rules the world and our lives.'

A year later, in December 1944, during his final Advent before his birth to eternal life, Bonhoeffer began to compose a poem in a prison cell under the Gestapo headquarters in Berlin. At this stage, he had already been in prison for almost two years, first on the outskirts of Berlin, then from October 1944 in the intimidating headquarters of the

Gestapo in the city centre. Things weren't bright and cheery for him, to say the least. The investigation had become so complex and entangled that his imprisonment dragged on and on. Meanwhile his fiancée had to cope with the reality that Bonhoeffer was in prison as a traitor to his nation, the same nation for which her own father and brother had died in battle on the Eastern Front. As for the Christian churches, they were in disarray, engulfed in the moral shame of having largely capitulated to the Nazis. The city of Berlin, where he was being held, experienced the constant pounding of Allied bomber planes. Yet, despite the gloominess of everything, Bonhoeffer wrote a poem that proclaimed his full trust in a loving God who was taking care of him.

This was Bonhoeffer's own 'Magnificat'. It's called 'By gracious powers' (*Von guten Mächten*). It's a forthright expression of full trust in God's presence at every time and in every circumstance, an unshakeable act of confidence that nothing can come between us and God's love. To end this section, and chapter, here is my free translation of the key stanza from this poem.

> *By gracious powers so wondrously surrounded,*
> *Standing trustingly, come what may.*
> *We know that God is with us night and morning*
> *And full of love he greets us each new day.*

CHAPTER TWO

MARY *in the* ORTHODOX CHRISTIAN WORLD

More honourable than the Cherubim,
And glorious incomparably more than the Seraphim.
Thou who inviolate did bring forth God the Word
And are indeed Mother of God.

The Liturgy of Saint John Chrysostom
(the most frequently celebrated form of the Divine Liturgy in the Orthodox churches)

An experiential faith

Orthodox Christians love Mary. They are fond of calling her by the name *Theotokos*. This Greek word is usually translated into English as the 'Mother of God' or 'God-bearer', and it gives us the key to how the Orthodox see Mary: they venerate her because she is God's mother in the full sense of the word. We're not talking merely about physical procreation. Mary was much more than the physical means that God used to take on human flesh: she was the one who gave God his human nature. This entails a vitally important affective and spiritual dimension. There is something unique about God's relationship to Mary: although he is her Lord and Saviour, Jesus is also her Son. And she is his mother. No one else has ever had that kind of relationship with the Son of God.

The incarnation – the astonishing reality that God gave up his privileges to come into our world as an utterly defenceless child – is of huge importance for Orthodox Christians. It is the key turning point in human history. And Mary is indelibly associated with this mystery, which is why the incarnation is traditionally depicted in Orthodox icons by two figures: the child Jesus and his mother Mary. It is quite natural for Orthodox Christians to venerate not only the Son of God, but also the creature in whom he took flesh through the power of the Holy Spirit – Mary. Indeed, Mary herself, while she was carrying Jesus in her womb, predicted this future veneration, announcing in the Magnificat that 'from now on all generations will call me blessed'. Orthodox believers confirm the truth of Mary's own prophecy through the way they lovingly venerate her.

In the West, we do not have a gut sense of how important the incarnation is for those of the Orthodox faith. We do not realise that for Orthodox Christians, the incarnation is not just a sideshow that precedes the main happening, the crucifixion. The incarnation is vitally important in itself; it is not just a preliminary step that led Jesus to the cross. That is because we are not saved by an event – the crucifixion, but by a person – Jesus Christ. And Christ didn't just die; he also lived. So the Orthodox eagerly embrace the whole story of Christ's existence among us, and not just his final harrowing hours on the cross. And so it is not all about Christ's death; instead it is all about Christ. And of course the Risen Christ is pivotal, because the Resurrection of Christ is the core and crown of Orthodox Christianity. Mary was all about Christ and all her life was about Christ.

Unlike the Roman Catholic and Protestant Churches, Orthodox Christians do not work out their theology in learned books or articles. Instead, they express it in the hymns and prayers of their liturgies, and in the icons that adorn their churches. Orthodox theology is 'caught', not 'taught'. What do you catch when you enter an Orthodox Church? Because of the heavy smell of incense, you could catch a fit of sneezing! An Orthodox liturgy is a feast for the senses: not only the incense, but also the rich colours of the icons on the walls, the glow of the priest's vestments and the sound of the chanting. An Orthodox liturgy is also a continual flow of movement, because no one really stays still: people are continually making the sign of the cross, bowing to the ground in adoration, and walking around the church to kiss the icons and light candles. The differences between the Orthodox and Catholic ways of doing things are especially apparent in the area of liturgy. For the Orthodox, the liturgy – worship in common – is at the heart of everything. For Catholics, the liturgy, although fundamental, is not lived in practice as though it were such a momentous and life-changing reality.

There is an interesting contrast between what Orthodox authorities say to the world publicly about Mary and how the Orthodox faithful act privately towards her within the sphere of their own faith. The Orthodox Churches do not give Mary a prominent place in their array of dogmas. However, this public reserve is not an indication of coldness or indifference, because in the day-to-day life of Orthodox believers,

Mary plays a crucial role. Ultimately the most powerful dimension of any church's life is not to be found at the public level of the values it espouses before the world, but at the deeper level of the core beliefs that shape the thoughts, words and deeds of its members. The Catholic Church publicly highlights the importance of Mary, but despite the greater reticence to be found in the official teaching of Orthodoxy, Eastern Christians seem to cherish Mary as much, and at times more, than Catholics do.

Here is a relatively recent example of the public prominence the Catholic Church gives to Mary: in 1950, it solemnly proclaimed the dogma of the Assumption, which says that at the end of her earthly life, Mary was assumed, body and soul, into heaven. In relation to this same core belief, the Orthodox world has never made any formal doctrinal proclamation. However, at the same time, it has clung passionately and tenaciously to this truth. It may not be a truth that the Orthodox world shouts from the rooftops, but for all that it is a truth that matters hugely to it, and so it shows itself in the way that the Orthodox practise their faith. So although the Orthodox Churches have never proclaimed Mary's Assumption (which they prefer to call the 'Dormition' or 'Falling Asleep') as a dogma, they actually celebrate the annual feast with genuine fervour. Although at the level of official teaching they might not seem to 'talk the talk' as the Catholic Church does, at the level of lived life they certainly 'walk the walk'. That is because the Orthodox are emotionally invested in Mary in a deep and sustained way. Their immense love for Mary becomes evident through attending an Orthodox liturgy. By simply observing the physical layout of the church, the many Marian icons that decorate it, and the emotions on people's faces as they venerate icons of the *Theotokos*, you can already tell a lot about how much Mary means for them. The Greek word *Theotokos*, which may sound theoretical to our ears, is anything but highbrow for the Orthodox. It is instead a term of endearment and affection. Orthodox Christianity is convinced that the human mind cannot understand mysteries as sublime as the person of Mary, so the way to her is the way of the heart.

Georges Florovsky, the twentieth-century Russian Orthodox priest and theologian, described the mysteriousness of Mary like this: 'The intimate experience of the Mother of the Lord is hidden from us. Nobody was ever able to share this unique experience, by the very nature of the case. It is the mystery of the person. This accounts for the dogmatic reticence of the Church in Mariological doctrine. The Church speaks of her rather in the language of devotional poetry, in the language of … metaphors and images.'

There are many icons of Mary and the child Jesus in Orthodox churches. Her name crops up time after time in Orthodox prayers and hymns, and Orthodox Christians turn to her for help at key moments in their lives. The Orthodox Church doesn't hand on its beliefs about Mary through doctrines or theology, but through the liturgy. This doesn't mean that Mary is relegated to the margins, because the truth is that the whole identity of the Orthodox Church is tied up with the liturgy. It is the source and fountain of holiness: everything streams from it. The liturgy is the living experience of what faith is all about, and not only faith, but life as a whole. While the Catholic Church has a more cerebral approach that spells out the role of Mary in dogmatic statements and theological formulations, the Orthodox Church has a more communal and mystical approach that venerates Mary in the context of gathering together to worship God, which is the fundamental purpose of Orthodox Christianity.

Mount Athos
The Orthodox love for Mary extends back through the centuries, and this enduring affection is particularly evident in the spiritual capital of Orthodox Christianity, Mount Athos. This spectacular peninsula in northern Greece is a little more than fifty kilometres long and on average ten kilometres wide. It is home to twenty monasteries and about two thousand monks. Although Mount Athos is a peninsula, it was an island for a time: in the fifth century BC, Xerxes, King of Persia, cut a canal through it. Even though only the smallest traces of this canal remain today, Mount Athos still has the feel of an island, because it is cut off in various ways from the rest of Greece. Indeed, many pilgrims still think of it as an island, since they are only allowed to arrive there by sea.

Although women are banned from visiting this stunning peninsula that stretches out over thirty miles into the Aegean Sea, this restriction is not intended to demean women. It is more an indication of the weakness of the monks themselves rather than a sign of any resentment against women. One monk remarked that if women were to come to Mount Athos, most of his fellow monks would abandon this sacred place to get married. At the same time, although the monks leave behind all the women they know, their reward is a relationship with a particularly special woman: the Virgin Mary. That is because this monastic enclave, capped by Mount Athos, almost 7,000 feet high, is dedicated to the *Theotokos*. She is regarded as the true abbess of this holy mountain, where the way of life has changed little since the first monks settled here in the ninth century.

According to tradition, Mary was providentially led to Mount Athos when the ship in which she was travelling was blown off course. As the story goes, a number of years after the Resurrection of Jesus, Lazarus, the brother of Mary and Martha, invited the Virgin Mary to visit the island of Cyprus. Contrary winds turned the ship from its intended route, and it came to shore on the eastern part of Athos, not far from where the monastery of Iviron is located today. There was a pagan temple there at the time, but when Mary set foot on the soil of Athos, the pagan idols called on the inhabitants to go forth to meet the Mother of God. The people of this area became Christian as a result. Mary was so taken by the wondrous beauty of this mountainous landscape that she prayed to her Son, asking him to give her this territory as her own personal domain. Her prayer was answered, and ever since the inhabitants of Mount Athos have called it the Garden of the Mother of God. The monks are convinced that Mary has given them her special protection through the centuries. Saint Peter the Athonite, one of the earliest hermits of Mount Athos, attributed these words to the Virgin Mary: 'This is the mountain that I have chosen out of all the earth … I have consecrated it to be henceforth my dwelling: this is why people will call it the "Holy Mountain". All who shall come to live there after having decided to fight the battle against the common enemy of the human race will find me at their side throughout their lives. I will be their invincible aid, I will teach them what they must do and what they must avoid.'

Saint Serpahim of Sarov

Many monks who never lived on Mount Athos have also experienced the maternal care of Mary. Among them is the most beloved saint in all of Russian Orthodoxy: Saint Seraphim of Sarov, who lived from 1754 to 1833. He had a deep love for Mary that is exceptional even by Orthodox standards. Because of his mystical gifts as well as his ability to read minds and hearts, he is sometimes compared to Western saints such as Padre Pio. Seraphim died in January 1833 while kneeling in prayer before the icon of the Virgin of Tenderness, which he called the joy of all joys. The pages of the gospels lay open before him. He was a man of such deep prayer that his life became a prayer. He was praised for this by another saint, Pope John Paul II, in his *Crossing the Threshold of Hope*.

Saint Seraphim was helped by Mary in the most difficult moments of his life. At the age of ten, he fell seriously ill and his mother thought he would die, but he told her that the Mother of God had appeared to him in a dream and had promised she would heal him. A few days later there was a procession in his home town of Kursk and, when it began to rain, the faithful stopped in the large courtyard of his family's house to protect the icon of Our Lady of Kursk. His mother took advantage of this to bring down her sick boy who was healed on the spot.

When he became a young monk, he went overboard in his enthusiasm, keeping vigils late into the night and fasting severely during the day. As a result, he became seriously ill and had to take to his bed for three long years. One evening, as death approached, the Mother of God appeared to him in a sea of light, accompanied by the apostles Peter and John. She pointed to the sick monk and said to them, 'he is one of ours'. Then she touched him and he felt a surge of energy. The swelling on his hip burst and water flowed out. A scar remained for the rest of his days.

Saint Seraphim was filled with the unspeakable joy of the Holy Spirit, and something of the freedom of the Spirit characterised his way of living the monastic life. He didn't fit into neat categories. His life as a monk alternated between solitiude and community. He immersed himself in silence for many years, but in the latter part of his life he became a spiritual father to the constant stream of pilgrims who arrived at his door. He knew that the Holy Spirit cannot be contained. And the crucial thing is to allow the Holy Spirit to take charge so that it is no longer we who live, but Christ who lives in us.

Seraphim taught that our goal as Christians is to be filled with the Holy Spirit: 'The true aim of our Christian life is the acquisition of the Holy Spirit. As for fasts, and vigils, and prayer, and almsgiving, and every good deed done because of Christ, they are only the means of acquiring the Holy Spirit ... Of course, every good deed done because of Christ gives us the grace of the Holy Spirit, but prayer gives it to us most of all, for it is always at hand, so to speak, as an instrument for acquiring the grace of the Spirit. For instance, you would like to go to church, but there is no church or the service is over; you would like to give alms to a poor person, but there isn't one, or you have nothing to give ... you would like to do some other good deed in Christ's name, but either you have not the strength or the opportunity is lacking. This certainly does not apply to prayer. Prayer is always possible for everyone, rich and poor, noble and humble, strong and weak, healthy and sick, righteous and sinful.'

The Holy Spirit pours out his gifts upon everyone, and Seraphim did not regard holiness as the unique preserve of monks or contemplatives. He knew that we don't acquire the Holy Spirit through 'saying' lots of prayers or kissing lots of icons or lighting lots of candles. Instead we acquire the Holy Spirit through the kind of prayer that is heartfelt and genuine. Saint Seraphim gave this provocative example to drive his point home: 'You may judge how great the power of prayer is even in a sinful person, when it is offered wholeheartedly, by the following example from Holy Tradition. A desperate mother who had been deprived by death of her only son chanced to meet a harlot, still unclean from her last sin. She was touched so much by the mother's deep sorrow that she cried to the Lord: "Not for the sake of a wretched sinner like me, but for the sake of the tears of a mother grieving for her son and firmly trusting in Thy loving kindness and Thy almighty power, Christ God, raise up her son, O Lord!" And the Lord raised him up.'

Seraphim radiated a sense of peace. He urged people to use every means at their disposal to preserve peace of soul. His most well-known expression is: 'Acquire inner peace, and thousands around you will find salvation.' Because Our Lady reached out to Seraphim in the difficult moments of his life, he was able to see these trials with the eyes of faith, and so they paradoxically became a source of peace and serenity for him. While he was living as a hermit, he was attacked one day by robbers who had heard rumours of treasure hidden in his simple hut. They beat him until he was unconscious, but when they searched his hut they found nothing except stones and potatoes. Somehow he dragged himself back to the monastery. While there he went into ecstasy. He saw the Mother of God with Peter and John, just as had happened during his illness as a young monk. Once again Mary said to Peter and John, 'he is one of us'. Seraphim felt huge comfort, though his full convalescence took several months. Although he was lame and hunched over for the rest of his life, he forgave his attackers. When they were found, he insisted that they should not be punished for their crime.

No matter what the season, Seraphim greeted people with the expression 'Christ is risen, my joy!' And with that greeting, something of the joy of the resurrection entered their hearts. The resurrection is central in the Orthodox faith. And the resurrection is not so much an event as a person. Jesus said, 'I am the resurrection and the life' (Jn 11:25). I like Saint Seraphim's habit of giving this upbeat greeting all year round, and not just during the Easter season. Whenever we feel discouraged, we can remind ourselves that Christ is risen, and that we are risen with him; and because of this we can give our worries to God and live in trust. Whenever we feel the downward pull of our own shortcomings and weaknesses, we can remind ourselves that Christ is risen, and that we are rising higher and higher with him each day. Since Mary knew and believed that Jesus would rise, she can help us to live in this joy of the resurrection.

This effort to unite ourselves to the resurrection of Christ makes a lot of sense from the Orthodox perspective. Orthodox icons of the resurrection (or *anastasis*, literally 'rising up') generally depict Christ pulling up Adam and sometimes Eve by the hand. At times other biblical figures are present as well. In other words, Orthodox icons depict a Resurrection that occurs for our sake, so that we too can rise up and live a new life. In the West, by contrast, the image of the resurrection (and it is often not displayed in our churches!) usually depicts Christ on his own, though sometimes there are sleeping guards shown at the tomb. So, while the Eastern Churches give us a sense of the universal and indeed cosmic significance of the resurrection, the Western Churches generally show only an individual resurrection. Orthodox Christianity can teach us how to live joyfully in the generous and vast horizons of the resurrection.

Divinisation

Orthodoxy does not honour Mary only because she gave birth to Jesus and reared him. It honours her most of all because she listened to the word and made it her own. We cannot imitate Mary by giving physical birth to Jesus, but we can imitate her by opening ourselves up completely to God. Honouring Mary as the God-bearer means honouring her example of utter openness to God. Mary welcomed God into her body and into her life. She incarnates then in a special way the huge possibilities that result from the fruitful encounter between divine grace and human freedom. Mary freely gave her assent to God so that he could realise his magnificent and loving plan of becoming one of us. She exemplifies the new kind of human being.

For the Orthodox, Mary's complete surrender led to *theosis*, or divinisation or deification. These terms are not used so frequently in the Catholic Church, for fear of causing confusion. But *theosis* is used again and again by the Orthodox, because divinisation is a pervasive motif in Orthodox spirituality. Deification or *theosis* was a term already used by Saint Gregory of Nazianzus in the fourth century. Even though it sounds like an unreachable goal, divinisation is in fact the destiny of every human being. Divinisation does not mean that we turn into God. We shall always remain creatures. We are never going to morph into God's equals. There is an infinite difference between the Creator and the creature, a difference that can never be annulled. We continue to be human beings, but, as Saint Peter puts it in his second letter, we become 'partakers of the divine nature' (2 Pet 1:4). Yet despite sharing in God's nature, we still remain radically different from God: for instance, God has no beginning and no end (he is eternal), whereas we have a beginning and no end (we are immortal). Divinisation doesn't mean that we lose our own identity by becoming absorbed into God, as sugar dissolves into tea. But it does mean that we can be lifted up by grace into something that we could never arrive at by ourselves: the very life of the Trinity. Saint Paul points out that the process of divinisation begins in this life. It gathers momentum as we become more and more like Christ: 'And we all, who with unveiled faces contemplate the Lord's glory, are being transformed into his image with ever-increasing glory, which comes from the Lord, who is the Spirit' (2 Cor 3:18).

It is the incarnation that makes *theosis* possible. Because Jesus shares our nature, we can be one with him. And because Jesus also enjoys the fullness of divine life, we too can share in God's own life. As Saint Irenaeus of Lyons expressed it in the second century, God became what we are so that we could become what God is. In the eyes of the Orthodox, Mary is the supreme example of a divinised creature, of a human being who is a living icon or image of God.

Mary as Icon

Icons are ubiquitous in Orthodox Christianity. They possess a richness of meaning that can help illuminate something of the mystery of Mary. An icon is both a window and a door: a window inviting us to gaze heavenwards, and a door allowing us to enter into the deepest levels of our own being. For those of us from the West, these religious pictures painted on wood panels often appear unrealistic, primitive, flat and lacking in perspective. This is because we tend to look at them as though they were artistic works. However, icons are not painted to portray things that are physically beautiful, but rather to depict holiness. Icons do not serve the purposes of art, but are intended to glorify God and to serve the Church. Icon painters try to give external expression to an inner spiritual reality, and usher the viewer into the invisible sphere of the Spirit.

Icons are not intended to be realistic, and in order to look at them properly we must leave the assumptions of the realistic world behind us. For instance, the source of light in these paintings is the spiritual nature of a person or the light of Christ, but not the light of the sun. The way the face is depicted also speaks volumes. The eyes, ears, nose and mouth are portrayed as sense organs that are no longer used in a biological way but are now employed in a spiritual manner, thanks to the workings of divine grace. The eyes are usually large, denoting wisdom and spiritual vision. The nose can be thin, representing an ascetic disposition. The mouth is as a rule small, indicating that the person now veers toward silence and stillness. The ears are large, symbolising the readiness to listen to God's voice.

In Western Christianity, we rely, perhaps excessively, on the spoken and written word to communicate faith. In the Orthodox world, images are the preferred medium. In the West, by contrast, certain Christian denominations are openly suspicious of images. But in actual fact, the whole point of using words is that they evoke images. In the West, we sometimes speak of opening the Word or opening Scripture, because in fact we view biblical verses in a similar way to how the Orthodox view icons: as windows opening us to the mystery of God and as doors inviting us into our own spirit. At the same time, by neglecting images, we are left with words that have lost much of their power. That's because words themselves, although they evoke images, cannot rival the power of a visual image; which is why we say that a picture speaks a thousand words. Even a long written analysis of Mona Lisa's mystifying smile pales next to the power of the painting itself.

When I call Mary a living icon, I mean a number of things. She is a *bridge* between time and eternity, between the material and spiritual world, between creatures and God. She is a *living* icon, because she shares the spiritual energy of the God whom she represents in such a compelling way. The Orthodox regard icons as more than just ornate artworks, but as channels of grace. Mary too is a *channel* of grace. And just as the Orthodox do not venerate what appears on the icon, but the divine likeness of the person in the icon, so too the *Theotokos* is venerated for her likeness to God and her closeness to Jesus. The Orthodox venerate icons, just as they venerate Mary; but they only worship God.

Mary was a living icon most of all because she allowed God to 'paint' her life according to his design. She allowed the Divine Artist to create the masterpiece he had in mind. Mary freely and fully responded to the wishes of God. She was completely open, and this is one of the features of her relationship with God that is highlighted in Orthodoxy. Mary was ever ready to be taken beyond herself, to be clasped by the Holy Spirit, and to be drawn into the stream of God's love. She opened herself up to a process, the process of being transformed into the likeness of Christ. We sometimes hear phrases such as 'Become the best person you can'. But great as this prospect is, it pales in comparison to the prospect of being so thoroughly transformed that the form of Christ informs our whole life. And that thrilling prospect was Mary's destiny.

Beauty

What we see depends on where we are standing. And since beauty is so important in the Orthodox world, let me provide a beautiful example. If you stand outside the Saint Sophia Greek Orthodox Cathedral in Los Angeles, it looks like a large church with a relatively simple design. It is only when you walk inside that you will be struck (and even awestruck) by its dazzling beauty. Seventeen crystal chandeliers hang from the ceiling, each weighing almost 1,000 kilos. Along the two side walls are twelve enormous stained-glass windows portraying the twelve apostles. At the rear wall of the sanctuary there is a massive icon of the Virgin Mary with outstretched arms and the child Jesus in her bosom. She is welcoming the faithful to paradise, and a Greek inscription reads: 'This is the Gate of Heaven'.

It is not possible to see the true beauty of this gorgeous cathedral unless you are inside it. Mary too lived inside the mystery. If Mary had stood too far back, if she had examined everything in a cold and dispassionate way, she wouldn't have seen the radiance of it all. However, Mary was attuned to God; she was inside the cathedral, she was rooted and grounded in what was deepest within her. Mary was a true contemplative, and so she was receptive.

It can be tempting to stay outside the cathedral and regard God from a safe distance, and as a result he can end up appearing as unappealing as stained-glass windows do when we're standing outside on a dull day. Western Christianity has a rational, legal and practical mentality that likes to define truth in a clear and precise way. This means that even when we 'know' in our heads that God is love, it can still take years for this truth to seep down into our hearts. Eastern Christianity veers more toward the kind of mysticism that emphasises the personal encounter with truth, especially through the shared experience of worship and the contemplative veneration of icons.

It is surely telling that in the Orthodox world, the book that stands out after the Bible is the *Philokalia* (which literally means 'love of beauty' or 'love of the good'), a work of five volumes that gathers together spiritual texts spanning a period of over a thousand years. This compilation of wisdom focuses in a special way on the prayer of the heart. The Orthodox world is at home with the wavelength of the heart. It doesn't prioritise cerebral clarity. Orthodox theologians develop their theology with the help of icons, incense, worship and liturgical prayer. In order to cross the threshold of mystery, we could benefit, like the Orthodox, and like Mary, from opening ourselves to the beauty of Christ, and to the beauty of faith.

Hans Urs von Balthasar, the twentieth-century Swiss theologian, expressed well the forlornness of a world without beauty: 'In a world without beauty ... the good must also lose its attractiveness, the self-evidence of why it must be carried out. The human being stands before the good and asks why it must be done ... In a world that no longer has enough confidence in itself to affirm the beautiful, the proofs of the truth have lost their cogency. In other words, syllogisms may still dutifully clatter away like rotary presses or computers which infallibly spew out an exact number of answers by the minute. But the logic of these answers is itself a mechanism which no longer captivates anyone. The very conclusions are no longer conclusive.'

There is a beauty about Mary, a beauty highlighted in the Orthodox world. Over the centuries many Orthodox believers have spent long hours of stillness and prayer before icons of the Mother of God. They have spoken to Mary and listened to her as she spoke to them. They have held her hand and allowed her to take them by the hand. They have asked her help to compose their Magnificat, their own living testimony to the unexpected things God has done in their lives: how he raised them up when they were down, and also how he cast them down when their arrogance got the upper hand; how he filled them when they acknowledged their need for him, and how he sent them away empty when they thought they were self-sufficient; how he blessed them and their families, honouring the promises he made to their ancestors. Some of them were graced to enter into the fullness of the Magnificat, and its vision left them breathless. It blessed them with a new way of seeing God, the world and themselves, a vision that embraced everyone and spread a mantle of hope over all of humanity.

And as their final beautiful act, they uttered their own version of Mary's 'let it be done unto me according to your word'. With Mary at their side, they looked towards God with great trust, and even though they could not predict the future, they were brave enough to surrender themselves. They gave God their yes, the yes that only they could give him. And they asked the *Theotokos*, the Mother of God, the *Panagia*, the All-Holy One, to help them live out this yes in all its breadth and length and height and depth.

A closer relationship?

Orthodox Christians revere Mary as much – and in practice often more – than Catholics do. They have no earth-shattering differences with Catholics when it comes to Mary. So why do both faiths still seem so far apart? Principally because there is a lot of baggage from the past, and also big differences in the way each group lives out essentially similar beliefs. Because Catholicism is much bigger than Orthodoxy, it is not as conscious of these wounds from the past. A loose analogy closer to home would be the Irish awareness of the Easter Rising of 1916 as the key event leading to the foundation of the Irish state versus the British unawareness of that same event. (By the way, it is understandable that the Easter Rising was so peripheral for the British, since it happened when all their attention was focused on the First World War, during which almost one million British soldiers died).

In the case of Orthodox Christians, the difficult memories go back to the formal separation of the Christian West from the Christian East in 1054. These painful events still bother Orthodox Christians, but most Catholics have little awareness of this troubled past. And many Catholics don't have the opportunity to grow in awareness because they don't encounter Orthodox Christians on a daily basis. Four out of every five of the world's Orthodox Christians are in Russia and Central Europe.

Most of the world's Catholics live outside this geographical heartland of Orthodox Christianity, and so the limits of their lives don't allow them to see how much history separates our two faiths.

The millennium-long sense of alienation that the Orthodox feel should not be discounted. This sense of alienation is reinforced by differences in liturgy and worship. As a result, even if we resolved all the theological differences between our faiths tomorrow, the Orthodox would not be ready for unity with the Catholic Church. The real tensions between us are at the level of how we live in the present and how we remember the past. These tensions remind me of the famous line from James Joyce's *Ulysses*: 'History is a nightmare from which I am trying to awake.'

Our tensions are too long-standing and embedded for us to sort out on our own. Could a good mother resolve them? Maybe bringing our differences before Mary and asking for her intercession could heal us into hope. It's worth trying.

CHAPTER THREE

MARY *in her* JEWISH MATRIX

Behold, a virgin shall conceive, and bear a son,
and shall call his name Emmanuel.
Isaiah, Chapter 7, verse 14

The Jewish Mary

Mary was part of the Jewish people and grew up in the Jewish faith. Now, the fact that she was Jewish is not what made Mary great, just as being Irish or English is not an automatic ticket to excellence. What made Mary so impressive, as her cousin Elizabeth realised, was the depth of her faith: 'Blessed is she who has believed' (Lk 1:45). Nevertheless, Mary's Jewishness was an extremely important part of who she was. The Jewish nation is not just any nation but God's chosen people. As Jesus told the Samaritan woman at the well: 'Salvation comes from the Jews' (Jn 4:22). The name Jesus means 'God saves', and the one who saves was born of a Jewish woman called Mary, in Hebrew *Miryam*.

Mary's Jewish faith was truly important to her. It is clear from the Gospels that she devoutly observed rituals and feast days. She had Jesus circumcised eight days after his birth (Lk 2:21). She presented Jesus at the Temple forty days after his birth, both in order to offer Jesus to the Father, and also to be herself cleansed of legal impurity through offering 'a pair of doves or two young pigeons' (Lk 2:24). In addition, she and Joseph brought Jesus to Jerusalem every year for Passover (Lk 2:41). Mothers were not in fact required to make this journey, so the fact that Mary accompanied Joseph and Jesus on this lengthy journey annually shows the extent of her commitment.

Mary's faith was not simply external: she also had a deep prayer life. This is particularly evident in her song of praise, the Magnificat: scriptural verses flow spontaneously from her lips as she glorifies and thanks God. The many allusions to psalms and other biblical books show how thoroughly familiar Mary was with the Jewish Scriptures. There are few teenagers who could have so readily put together a hymn of the quality of the Magnificat, brimming over with poetry and praise. Indeed, perhaps the hymn came so easily to her lips because it was a constant refrain in her heart. In any event, it is clear that Mary was at home with the Scriptures. After she gives birth to Jesus and receives a visit from the shepherds, we glimpse a more contemplative side to her prayer life: we're told that she treasured all these things in her heart (Lk 2:19). After she finds Jesus in the Temple, Luke gives us almost the exact same phrase again, reaffirming how much Mary treasures everything in her heart (Lk 2:51). After the Ascension of Jesus, as the apostles await the outpouring of the Holy Spirit, Mary the contemplative prays with them in the upper room (Acts 1:16).

How can Judaism enable us see Mary anew? There is so much to say that a book would hardly be enough to skim the surface of it all. I'll limit myself to exploring how Mary had a deep sense of being chosen, how she saw herself as spiritually poor, how certain prophets allude to her, and why she can legitimately be called the Ark of the Covenant. But first I'll turn to four intriguing Jewish women in the Old Testament who can help us see Mary's outstanding qualities in a fresh light. The stories of three of these women – Sarah, Rebekah, and Rachel – are told in the Book of Genesis; the fourth – Esther – has a book named in her honour.

As for Eve, well, she wasn't Jewish. Adam and Eve lived at the dawn of humankind, and the Jewish people had not yet come into being, which is why Eve's name means 'mother of the living', and not just mother of one particular people or nation. But for all that, we will look at Eve in the context of discussing the first prophecy about Mary in Scripture, a prophecy in the third chapter of the Book of Genesis, which in fact implies that Mary will be the new Eve, the new mother of the living.

Strictly speaking, Judaism only began with the covenant on Mount Sinai, though in a looser sense, it started about four thousand years ago with Abraham, who lived sometime between 2100 BC and 1800 BC. God chose Abraham, made a covenant with him, and Abraham himself was committed to the central principle of the Jewish faith – that there is one God.

Sarah

If we take this covenant between God and Abraham as the starting point of Judaism, then Abraham's wife Sarah is the first Jewish woman. Sarah also has a maidservant Hagar with whom she has a problematic relationship.

While Jews see themselves as descendants of Abraham through Sarah's son Isaac, Muslims see themselves as descendants of Abraham through Hagar's son Ishmael. Sarah and Hagar, then, are the female figures at the origins of Judaism and Islam respectively. We'll see presently that Mary's relationship with her cousin Elizabeth is a healthy countersign to the dysfunctional relationship between Sarah and Hagar.

Although they are almost two thousand years apart, Mary is nonetheless conscious of her relationship to Sarah, and of its importance. In her Magnificat she extols God for the mercy he has promised to Abraham and his descendants, among whom she counts herself. Now, Abraham was only able to have these descendants because of Sarah. So, although Mary only mentions Abraham by name in her Magnificat, she is probably implicitly thinking of Sarah as well.

Initially Sarah and her husband were Sarai and Abram, but later, God gave them new names to indicate a new identity and destiny for them. Abram [exalted father] became Abraham [father of a multitude] and Sarai [particular or local princess, limited to a single family] became Sarah [princess of the nations]. The change in each of their names involved the addition of a single Hebrew letter, 'hey'. Although this seems like a tiny change, it is hugely significant. In the Hebrew language, the letter 'hey' appears twice in God's sacred name, so it is a symbol of his divinity. By adding this letter of his own name to their names, God was conferring something of his own spirit upon each of them. Mary also receives a new name when the angel Gabriel visits her in Nazareth. He doesn't call her Mary but 'full of grace', an expression which is conveyed by a single word in the original Greek of the New Testament – *kecharitomene* – because she is so full of God that there is no space in her heart for anything less than love.

Luke's story of the Annunciation to Mary and of her visit to Elizabeth is in some ways like the story of Sarah and her maidservant Hagar turned upside down. In the Gospel of Luke we witness the miracle of Elizabeth – old and barren – giving birth. In a similar way, Sarah – old and barren – miraculously gives birth, after God makes a covenant with Abram, renaming him and his wife and pouring out his blessings upon them. When God visits Abraham by the oak of Mamre in the guise of three men and promises that Sarah will have a son the following year, Sarah laughs in disbelief. As a result her son receives the name Isaac, which means 'he laughs'. Mary, though, believes the words of the angel, even though the promise made to her was much more extraordinary than the one made concerning Sarah, since it was not about healing barrenness but about a virgin conceiving through the power of the Holy Spirit.

Because Sarah is unable to conceive for many years, she gives Hagar to her husband so that Abraham can father a son with her. Because of the fractious relationship between Sarah and Hagar, the latter is sent into the desert with her son Ishmael. When the water runs out, Hagar becomes desperate. But God's angel reassures Hagar, saying, 'Do not be afraid', and she finds a source of water. The angel Gabriel says the same to Mary. And in her song of praise to God, Mary seems to call to mind many vulnerable people like Hagar, announcing that God has raised up the lowly and filled the hungry with good things.

On the one hand, Mary sees herself as poor and lowly, just like Hagar; on the other hand, she is the recipient of wonderful blessings, just like Sarah. Both Sarah and Mary receive unexpected promises in the midst of their ordinary lives. Through Isaac, Sarah will have innumerable descendants. Through Jesus, Mary will have innumerable descendants as well, all those who believe in her Son. For both women, giving birth is literally a once in a lifetime experience. For Sarah this is a first in two senses: it is her first (and only) child, but she is also the first in a long line of barren wives in the Bible whom God heals of infertility – and Mary's cousin Elizabeth will be the last in this line.

God chooses Sarah to bear a child at her advanced age in order to show that this birth is the work of God. It is a sign that God is the origin of the chosen people and the source of their fruitfulness. 'And by faith even Sarah, who was past childbearing age, was enabled to bear children because she considered him faithful who had made the promise. And so from this one man, and he as good as dead, came descendants as numerous as the stars in the sky and as countless as the sand on the seashore' (Heb 11:11–12).

Sarah is barren, and she becomes the mother of 'descendants as numerous as the stars in the sky'. Mary is vowed to virginity, and she becomes more fruitful than any other woman in history, bearing the Son of God himself. Both women are invited to believe with all their hearts. Sarah has to wait many years before the promise of a child is fulfilled. But although Mary does not have to wait a long time, she is asked to believe something that it would take more than a lifetime for most people to credit: that, while remaining a virgin, she will conceive. This is unheard of. But there's more. Mary is also asked to believe that the child she will conceive is going to be divine as well as human. This is really stretching faith to the limit. But Mary responds with her yes of love.

Sarah and Mary are both strong women. They don't give birth in ideal circumstances – Sarah is advanced in age; Mary has to give birth in the poverty of Bethlehem and shortly afterwards flee to Egypt. Yet they are not undermined by the difficulties they encounter. Through the births of their sons, they inaugurate something new for humanity. These two women are free enough to move forward from what they already know towards the unknown that God is promising them. They trust the God of surprises. They are true blessings for humanity.

Rebekah

After Sarah dies, Abraham sends his servant on a long journey to Mesopotamia to find a suitable wife for his son Isaac. At a well outside the city of Haran in Mesopotamia, the servant meets Rebekah, who is carrying a water jar on her shoulder. The Book of Genesis emphasises that Rebekah is a virgin before she marries Isaac, just as the Gospels of Matthew and Luke highlight Mary's virginity. Mary calls herself the servant of the Lord in response to Gabriel's invitation to give birth to the only-begotten Son. For her part, Rebekah shows her willingness to serve not only by giving water to Abraham's servant but also by volunteering to draw water for each of his ten camels – about 150 litres altogether! It is this blend of kindness, sensitivity, industry, and initiative that no doubt convinces Abraham's servant that Rebekah is the right woman for Isaac.

Rebekah leaves her family and homeland in order to travel to the land of her future husband. We are told that Isaac loves her, the first time in the Bible that this is said of a husband. Despite the newfound bliss of marriage, for twenty years Rebekah suffers from the same stigma that once afflicted her mother-in-law Sarah: she remains barren. She finally gives birth to twin boys.

Esau, the elder son, is Isaac's favourite, and becomes a hunter, a man who likes being out in the open fields, whereas Jacob, the younger son, is Rebekah's favourite, and stays closer to home. Isaac intends to give his blessing to Esau, so that the firstborn will be the principal beneficiary of everything. But Rebekah convinces her younger son Jacob to disguise himself as Esau in order to steal the blessing intended for the latter.

In his *Vie intérieure de la Très-Sainte Vierge*, Jean-Jacques Olier describes how Mary serves Jesus in his task of reconciling us with the Father, by helping to draw the Father's blessings upon us, just as Rebekah drew Isaac's blessing upon their younger son Jacob. Although not everyone would agree with his interpretation, it is thought-provoking. Olier describes how this happens at the foot of the cross, when Jesus, looking at the beloved disciple, says to Mary: 'behold your son'. Because of this, Mary sees all of us as beloved disciples, supporting Jesus as he offers us to the Father, and the Father now sees all of us as his adopted children. He pours out his blessings upon us, and redirects the punishment we deserve to Jesus. In this way, Jesus fulfils what Olier sees as the deepest meaning hidden within the story of Jacob and Esau.

Moreover, Olier suggests that Isaac, the father of Jacob and Esau, stands for God the Father, and Rebekah, their mother, born in the midst of the Gentiles, represents the Virgin Mary. On Calvary, Mary clothes us with the merits of Jesus, and presents us to the Father, just as Rebekah clothed Jacob in the garments of Esau, so that Jacob would receive Isaac's blessing. Since Mary clothes us with the merits of Jesus, the Father takes us for his beloved children.

Rachel

Rachel is the daughter-in-law of Rebekah. Her story can give us fresh insights into Mary's compassion for all who suffer. Although Rachel only gave birth to two of the twelve brothers who make up the nation of Israel, to this very day she is revered as the quintessential mother of all Israel. The mother of only two sons during her life, Rachel has become the mother of millions of Jews throughout history. In a similar way, although only giving physical birth to Jesus, Mary has become the mother of innumerable children through the centuries. Moreover, Rachel and Mary are women who suffered, and that is why so many believers turn so confidently to both of them in their moments of trial. They know that these most compassionate of women truly understand them.

As with her mother-in-law Rebekah, the first impression the Book of Genesis gives of Rachel is her striking beauty. Chapter 20 tells us that 'Rachel had a lovely figure and was beautiful'. She seems the kind of person whose life will be a breeze because everyone will be drawn to her on account of her captivating looks. However, her life turns out quite differently.

Her father compels Rachel to wait seven years to marry the man who loves her, Rebekah's son Jacob. Luckily for Rachel, Jacob is so deeply in love that these seven years of serving her father Laban 'seemed to him like a few days because of his love for her' (Gen 29:20). Even when these seven years are up, and the day of their wedding arrives, Rachel suffers the anguish of seeing her father inveigle Jacob into marrying her sister Leah instead. The next day Jacob confronts her father, who agrees to give his daughter Rachel to Jacob as well, on condition that Jacob works yet another seven years in his service.

Rachel doesn't bear any children for many years, which is even more humiliating, because meanwhile her sister Leah bears six sons to Jacob. Eventually, Rachel gives birth to Joseph, and a time of joy follows. But when she goes into labour with her second son, she undergoes intense pain and dies giving birth to a boy whom she calls Ben-Oni, or 'son of my affliction'. After her death, Jacob changes his name to Benjamin, which means 'son of my right hand'.

Rachel isn't buried where Sarah and Rebekah are buried, at the tomb of the patriarchs and other matriarchs in Hebron, but alone in a tomb on the road to Bethlehem. Yet despite this lonely wayside location, her tomb is regarded as one of the holiest sites in Judaism. For centuries, Jews have come here to pour out their hearts to her. The fact that she is in this isolated place has not deterred them, but has in fact drawn them, because it seems to them she has deliberately chosen to be there in order to be more accessible to all the suffering children of her people.

We are familiar with the poignant quotation about Rachel in the Gospel of Matthew at the time of King Herod's slaughter of male children in and around Bethlehem: 'Then what was said through the prophet Jeremiah was fulfilled: A voice is heard in Ramah, weeping and great mourning, Rachel weeping for her children and refusing to be comforted, because they are no more' (Mt 2:18).

It is important to note that Rachel did not lose either of her two children: she was the one who died first, not them. So this verse is obviously *not* saying that Rachel is weeping for her own biological children. Moreover, the Gospel of Matthew is not quoting from the Book of Genesis, which tells the story of Rachel's life, but from the prophet Jeremiah. As it turns out, Jeremiah isn't referring to Rachel's life at all, but to a key moment in the history of the Jewish people: the exile in Babylon.

After the Babylonians destroyed Jerusalem, they marched the captives out of the city, and, as they began the long trek to Babylon, their route apparently passed by Rachel's tomb, which is only a few miles south of Jerusalem. The people were weeping, and Rachel, although buried in a tomb, was somehow weeping with them. She was spiritually and emotionally present to them. She was a comfort to the people who were about to face seventy years of exile. They knew that she cared. They knew they had a compassionate mother in Rachel. She was someone who had suffered herself, waiting years to marry the love of her life, enduring barrenness for many years of her marriage, and never experiencing the joy of seeing her sons grow up before her eyes. Jewish mothers still flock to Rachel's tomb in the sure knowledge that she will make their burden lighter.

Mary suffered hugely on account of the suffering and death of Jesus, and not just because he was her own son. More than anyone else, Mary was aware of his true dignity. She knew he was God as well as man. She knew better than anyone else the immensity of his perfections. She knows our own dignity better than we do ourselves. She is conscious of the true grandeur of every person, and this makes her extraordinarily sensitive to any human suffering. Her vast reservoir of sympathy means she can be a listening and healing presence to anyone undergoing difficulties. She is the comforter of the afflicted.

Esther

Esther took action to save her people from destruction. This simple truth helps us to see Mary in a new light. There is a tendency to regard Mary as passive or, worse still, as a doormat. But if we put the story of Esther side by side with Mary's Annunciation, we realise that Mary is not merely the passive recipient of the message of the angel. Mary knew that God wanted to send his only Son among us so that whoever believed in him might have eternal life. The salvation of the world was at stake. Something had to be done; action had to be taken; and it was up to her to do it. And she was ready to do what God asked of her to make salvation possible.

Esther's role is celebrated annually in the Feast of Purim, one of the most joyful Jewish holidays. The festival is marked by the public reading of the Book of Esther in the synagogue, the giving of gifts of food to friends, the distribution of alms to the poor, and participation in a festive meal. In fact, there is so much partying, feasting and dressing up involved that this holiday has been dubbed the 'Jewish Mardi Gras'. The Talmud, a text that includes a compendium of Jewish religious law, goes so far as to prescribe that someone should drink so much alcohol on the Feast of Purim that he no longer knows the difference between 'cursed be Haman' (the villain of the story) and 'blessed be Mordecai' (the hero of the story).

The story behind this Jewish holiday unfolds in ancient Persia. Orphaned at a young age, Esther is raised by her cousin Mordecai. When the wife of the King of Persia publicly disobeys the king, he banishes her and initiates a search for a new queen. The most beautiful girls in Persia are brought to the palace, where they attend a kind of finishing school for a year, after which they are presented before the king. Enraptured by Esther's beauty, King Ahasuerus selects her from all the candidates, places a crown upon her head, and makes her queen. At Mordecai's insistence, Esther keeps her Jewish identity secret, even after becoming queen. Soon Mordecai gets into trouble for repeatedly refusing to bow before Haman, the highest-ranking official in the kingdom. Haman resolves to kill not only Mordecai, but also all the Jews in Persia. The king gives him carte blanche. Haman casts lots – *purim* in Hebrew, hence the name of this feast – to choose a date for the annihilation of the Jewish people, the thirteenth day of the month of Adar.

Mordecai sends word of the impending annihilation of the Jews to his cousin Esther, begging her to intercede with the king. Esther is highly reluctant to do so, because anyone who approaches the king without being summoned can be punished with death. Mordecai argues that if Esther does nothing, sooner or later her own life will be in danger: he explains that no Jewish person, even in the royal palace, is safe. If she fails to act, he predicts that deliverance will come from elsewhere, but before this happens, she and her family name will be wiped out. Ultimately he suggests that Esther may be queen for a preordained purpose: to save her people precisely at this decisive moment. Although Esther may not feel she's cut out for this daunting task, something has to be done and she is the only one in a position to do it.

Mordecai's final reason reminds me of an exchange early in J.R.R. Tolkien's *The Lord of the Rings*, where the hobbit Frodo is feeling weighed down by the burden of carrying a ring that brings evil in its wake, and could lead to his death. He says: 'I wish it need not have happened in my time.' And the wise wizard Gandalf replies: 'So do all who live to see such times; but that is not for them to decide. All we have to decide is what to do with the time that is given to us.'

Mordecai's reasons convince Esther. She asks him to gather all the Jews in the town of Susa and to fast for three days. She does the same. Then she goes to the king, even though she risks death by turning up unannounced. But the king displays a surprisingly indulgent side to his nature, going so far as to offer her whatever she wants, even half his kingdom. She asks the king to come with Haman to a banquet she has prepared. Once that is over, she asks that they come to another banquet the following day. At this second banquet, Esher reveals that she and her people are to be annihilated by none other than Haman. The king is incensed; with appropriate irony, he ensures that Haman is hanged on the very gallows that the latter had prepared for Mordecai.

Mary and Esther
By placing Esther's story alongside that of Mary, we get a better sense of Mary's strength and courage. Esther is a heroine for the Jewish people; Mary is a heroine for Christians. Esther lived in a royal palace; Mary lived in a little town in Galilee. Esther was identified by her relative Mordecai as the person to save her people; God chose Mary. The angel Gabriel tells Mary that she has found favour with God, and that she has been chosen out of all the women in the world to give birth to the Son of God.

Esther takes a big risk by daring to approach the king unannounced; Mary's big risks become evident over time. The first risk is this huge yes to God's invitation. How will this pregnancy affect her fiancé? What will happen when he discovers she is with child? There is the risk of death by stoning; or, if he leaves her quietly, the struggle of rearing her child alone, stigmatised and excluded by the village culture around her.

Immediately after giving her yes to God, Mary travels a hundred miles to visit her cousin Elizabeth. At that time, women, whether single or married, were not allowed to travel without a chaperone. But Mary, filled with the urgency of a sense of mission, makes haste to the hill country of Judea to be of service. When Mary herself is almost due, she travels with Joseph from Nazareth to Bethlehem, and gives birth to Jesus in an unwelcoming stable. The very day she presents Jesus in the Temple, Simeon tells her in no uncertain terms that her life will include a huge amount of sorrow – a sword will pierce her soul. It's like the second phase of the Annunciation, as the momentous consequences of her yes become ever more starkly revealed. She flees to Egypt at the shortest of notice ... The risks continue to accumulate over time, until she has to do something no one would wish on any mother: be present as her beloved child is tortured, crucified and buried in a cold tomb.

Esther interceded for her people; Mary does the same. Indeed, it already happens during the lifetime of Jesus. At the wedding feast at Cana, Mary notices that the guests have run out of wine. She asks Jesus to do something for them. Over the centuries, countless Christians who have run out of wine – out of energy, out of joy and out of resources – have turned to Mary, imploring her to intercede with God on their behalf.

By the way, when it comes to Mary's intercession, there is potential for misunderstanding between Catholics and Protestants. When Catholics speak about prayer, we often mean asking for something in an earnest and humble way. When we pray to Mary, we are asking her to help us. Sometimes other Christians presume that by praying to Mary we are in effect worshipping or adoring Mary. The truth is that we honour her, as a charitable organisation honours someone who has procured a significant donation from a wealthy benefactor. Just as the help of a well-placed friend on earth makes a difference, the help of a proven friend in heaven makes an even greater difference.

The Queen Mother

We have just looked at the intercession of Queen Esther. We can also learn about Mary's intercessory power with her Son by reflecting on another figure from the Old Testament: the Queen Mother. The First Book of Kings names many queen mothers in the kingdom of Judah, women who had a much higher and more influential role in the affairs of state than the wives of monarchs. An excellent example is Bathsheba, King David's wife and the mother of Solomon. In the first chapter of the First Book of Kings, she approaches her husband King David to make a request of him. She is extremely deferential. She bows in homage to the king. It is obvious that in relation to the king, even though he is her husband, she has little authority. As though to reinforce her inferior position, David's response borders on rudeness: 'What do you want?' Contrast this with the second chapter of the same book. David has now died, and Solomon has become king. In relation to her son Solomon, Bathsheba is the queen mother. She comes into the presence of King Solomon to make a request of him. What happens? Solomon stands up when *she* enters, *he* bows and pays *her* homage. He provides a throne for *her*, sits *her* at his right, and then invites her to make her request. It is an extraordinary contrast with the previous chapter when she was 'only' a queen. In this second chapter of the First Book of Kings, we see a new institution being born: the queen mother or great lady, known in Hebrew as *gebirah*. The queen mother does not usurp the role of the king: note that she does not sit on his throne, but at his right. And although Solomon bows in homage to Bathsheba, he doesn't stop being king because of this. Nevertheless, as queen mother, Bathsheba has a unique position of authority and influence with the king. He is in charge, but for all that he has not forgotten the ties of affection and respect that bind him to his mother.

The question could be asked: why does Solomon give this influential role to his mother and not to his wife? The problem was that he had 700 wives, a statistic that both beggars belief and appears morally reprehensible. Certain scholars have defended him by claiming that given heavy battle casualties, there would have been many more women than men, and marriage to Solomon at least offered these women some form of security; but this is to ignore the fact that the reign of Solomon, unlike that of his father David, was relatively free of war. In any event, had Solomon chosen one of his wives for this influential position, how would he have justified this choice and explained it to the other 699 women? It would have been a diplomatic and affective minefield, to say the least. However, Solomon only ever had one mother, so there was no problem about choosing her, since she was the only eligible candidate.

If we keep this figure of the queen mother in mind, it helps us to see Mary's role at Cana with new eyes. The scene is a wedding. Mary notices they have run out of wine. She tells Jesus. But why should she be the one to take the initiative? After all, it isn't her house, and she isn't the mother of the bridegroom. She is only one of the many guests. Crucially, she knows her son is king in the most exalted sense of that word. This means that she is the queen mother, and so she has the confidence to step up and make a request of him. It's not that she sees herself as having a right by virtue of being his natural mother; it is rather that being his mother gives her unparalleled access to Jesus.

When Mary tells Jesus that they have run out of wine, he replies to her as a monarch might speak to his subject: 'Woman, what is there between you and me?' But for all that, he still follows her suggestion. As for Mary, she has no intention of usurping his rightful place; she knows that Jesus occupies the true seat of authority, so she simply says to the servers, 'Do whatever he tells you'. In other words, they shouldn't obey her, but Jesus.

Mary and the Ark of the Covenant

The Ark of the Covenant is described in the Book of Exodus as a wooden chest covered in gold, and holding the two stone tablets upon which are written the Ten Commandments. This ark can tell us a lot about Mary. Just as the ark contained the tablets of the Law and some manna, so Mary carries within her womb the living Law and the Bread of Life.

The key thing about the ark is the fact that God's presence dwelt within it. The ark vanished in the sixth century BC, around the time the Babylonians invaded Jerusalem, destroyed the Temple and made the people captive in Babylon. Its disappearance is still a source of intrigue: the search for the lost ark provided the plot for one of the highest-grossing films of all time, the 1981 action adventure, *Raiders of the Lost Ark*.

However, if the New Testament is to be believed, the ark may not have disappeared at all; instead it may simply have moved location from an inanimate chest of acacia wood to a living person. When we carefully read key passages in the New Testament, especially the account of Mary's visit to her cousin Elizabeth, the signs point to Mary as the new Ark of the Covenant.

The Annunciation already hints at a link between the Ark of the Covenant and Mary. Recall that in the final chapter of the Book of Exodus, God orders Moses to set up the tabernacle of the tent of meeting and to place the Ark of the Covenant in it. We're told that 'the cloud covered the tent of meeting and the glory of the Lord filled the tabernacle' (Ex 40:34). In other words, God covers the tent of meeting from above and the tabernacle from within. In Luke's Gospel, Gabriel tells Mary: 'the Holy Spirit will come upon you, and the power of the Most High will overshadow you' (Lk 1:35). The Holy Spirit will come down upon Mary, while Jesus will fill her with his presence from within.

But the really fascinating parallels between the ancient Ark of the Covenant and Mary are to be found in the account of Mary's visit to her cousin Elizabeth. When Elizabeth welcomes her cousin, her words echo those of King David at the coming of the old ark. King David asks: 'How can the ark of the Lord come to me? (2 Sam 6:9). Elizabeth asks: 'How is it granted to me, that the mother of my Lord should come to me?'(Lk 1:43). David dances with abandon before the ark (2 Sam 6:14); the child in Elizabeth's womb leaps for joy at the presence of Jesus within Mary's womb (Lk 1:46).

In David's time, the ark remained in a house in the hill country of

Judah for three months and God blessed the house as a result (2 Sam 6:11). In a similar way, Mary remains for three months in the house of Elizabeth, also in the hill country of Judah, and Elizabeth more than once describes Mary as blessed. Mary brings blessings to Elizabeth and to her household, which are certainly needed, not only given Elizabeth's pregnancy at her advanced age, but also because Elizabeth's husband, the priest Zechariah, has been struck dumb in the Temple because he hasn't believed the promise of the angel Gabriel.

Another episode in Luke's Gospel also alludes to the Ark of the Covenant. When Mary and Joseph bring Jesus to the Temple for the presentation, the old man Simeon takes Jesus into his arms, saying that he can now die in peace since he has seen 'the glory of your people Israel' (Lk 1:32). The Temple had lost the indwelling presence of God (called *Shekinah* in Hebrew) after the disappearance of the Ark of the Covenant. Now, once again, Simeon senses the grace of God's presence, thanks to Mary.

The old ark held the law of God inscribed on stone tablets. The new ark, Mary, holds God himself, in the flesh. As the Catechism of the Catholic Church puts it, commenting on the angel Gabriel's greeting to Our Lady: 'Mary, in whom the Lord himself has just made his dwelling, is the daughter of Zion in person, the ark of the covenant, the place where the glory of the Lord dwells' (n. 2676).

Prophetic signs of Mary

In the first book of the Bible, there is a fascinating and mysterious prophecy. It is given when three figures are summoned before God in the Garden of Eden: Adam, Eve and the serpent. Although Mary's name is not mentioned, she has been traditionally linked with this prophecy. It is pronounced immediately after the sin of Adam and Eve. God says to the serpent: 'I will put enmity between you and the woman, and between your offspring and hers. They will crush your head, while you will strike at their heel' (Gen 3:15). Based on the words 'they will crush your head', this statement has been described as the 'first gospel' or *protoevangelium*, since already, in these initial moments after the fall of Adam and Eve, God opens up a beacon of hope, giving the first couple a glimmer of future salvation. In order to encourage Adam and Eve, God guarantees victory: the serpent's head will be crushed.

The serpent in question isn't an actual reptile. He doesn't use venom or asphyxiating force to hurt Adam and Eve. He employs his intelligence.

And he proves to be smarter – and more devious – than they are. He has traditionally been identified as Satan. A serpent is an appropriate animal to symbolise Satan: on the one hand, a serpent is rarely seen; on the other hand, it slithers and slides everywhere. Its mere presence causes fear, while its venom can lead to a painful death. Not only is the serpent more intelligent than Adam and Eve; he is also more blameworthy. He knows what he is doing. He knows the difference between good and evil; and he incites them to rebel against God's command. And because he is guiltier than they are, he is also the first to be punished by God, and the only one to be cursed: 'cursed are you' (Gen 3:14). God is more indulgent toward Adam and Eve, since he knows they have sinned out of weakness, not malice. He predicts an enmity that will rage between the offspring of the serpent (those who follow what Satan insinuates) and the woman's offspring.

God intended Adam and Eve to stay in a close relationship with him and not to taste death. The serpent robs them of divine intimacy and personal immortality. They walked with God in the Garden of Eden: now they will be banished from this garden; life and happiness stretched out endlessly before them; now they will be subject to disease, decline and death. Since the serpent has opposed God's plan for Adam and Eve, he is not only their enemy, but also an enemy of God himself. The ruptured relationship between God and the first couple will affect their descendants as well, and so it won't be easily healed. It will require a special person who can triumph over the serpent in the name of all, a person whose triumph will be decisive enough to satisfy God.

This special person will be the Messsiah. Jesus will inaugurate a new Genesis, a new beginning for humanity. The Messiah will battle against the serpent and crush the serpent's head, but in the process, the Messiah's heel will be struck; Jesus will suffer and die.

Mary's involvement is not clearly stated, but it is hidden in these words of God to the serpent: 'I will put enmity between you and the woman'. God could have said, 'between you and the man', because he is pointing above all towards the hope of the future Messiah. Instead he says, 'between you and the woman'. The woman in question obviously isn't Eve, because she has just gone along with the serpent and rebelled against God's commandment. There is no enmity beween Eve and the serpent.

This woman to whom God is referring will be a woman clearly opposed to the serpent. Just as Eve is Adam's companion, this other woman will be the companion of Christ, the new Adam, and so she will be the new Eve. Just as the first Eve played a significant role in the Fall, the new Eve will play an important role in Redemption. Just as the first Eve is mother of the living in a biological way, the new Eve will be mother of the living in a spiritual manner. As the first Eve was created immaculate and without stain of original sin, the second Eve will also be created pure and immaculate.

Two women in the Old Testament stand out for having crushed the heads of enemies: Jael and Judith. The Book of Judges tells the story of Jael, a humble Bedouin woman who became an unlikely heroine. She took on Sisera, the general of the Canaanite army, and defeated him singlehandedly. When the Canaanite commander drifted off to sleep in her tent, she took a tent peg and hammer, and drove the peg through his skull. His head was crushed, and the nation was saved. The prophetess Deborah praised Jael with words that anticipate the praise Elizabeth bestows on Mary. She said: 'Most blessed of women is Jael... blessed among tent-dwelling women' (Jg 5: 24).

The Book of Judith tells the story of Judith, a beautiful widow from the city of Bethulia who cut off the head of Holofernes, the general of the Assyrian army. She used his own sword as he lay in a drunken stupor on his bed. She returned home to Bethulia with his head in a bag. When she took his head out of the bag and showed it to the citizens, the magistrate Uzziah hailed her with words that again anticipate Elizabeth's praise of Mary: 'Blessed are you, daughter, by the Most High God, above all the women on earth' (Jdt 13:18).

The Jews were saved from their foes on account of the courage of these two women, Jael and Judith. Apart from Jael and Judith, only one other woman in the entire Bible is called 'blessed', and that woman is Mary. What all three women have in common, and what makes each one of them blessed, is that they have conquered a fierce enemy. In the case of Jael and Judith, the enemy is a human enemy: Jael crushed the head of the general of the Canaanites, and Judith cut off the head of the general of the Assyrians. In Mary's case, it is a spiritual enemy. Mary crushes the head of the commander of evil and sin. Her unconditional yes to God opens the way for the Word to become flesh. It is because of her assent that victory over the devil becomes possible. The incarnation delivers the decisive and fatal blow to the forces of evil, for Mary gives the world its Saviour.

Early Christian saints were intrigued by the contrasts between Eve and Mary. Saint Irenaeus of Lyons, martyred about AD 200, contrasts Eve and Mary like this: 'As Eve was seduced by the word of an angel and so fled from God after disobeying his word, Mary in her turn was given the good news by the word of an angel, and bore God in obedience to his word. As Eve was seduced into disobedience to God, so Mary was persuaded into obedience to God; thus the Virgin Mary became the advocate of the virgin Eve.'

Saint John Chrysostom, the archbishop of Constantinople who died in exile in AD 407, wrote: 'A virgin, a tree and a death were the symbols of our defeat. The virgin was Eve: she had not yet known man; the tree was the tree of the knowledge of good and evil; the death was Adam's penalty. But behold again a Virgin and a tree and a death, those symbols of defeat, become the symbols of his victory. For in place of Eve there is Mary; in place of the tree of the knowledge of good and evil, the tree of the Cross; in place of the death of Adam, the death of Christ.'

In medieval times, Christian thinkers and mystics such as Saint Hildegard of Bingen liked to play with the two Latin words *ave* (hail) and *Eva* (Eve). They remarked that the angel Gabriel's *ave* to the Virgin Mary was the exact reverse of the name *Eva*, just as Mary's affirmation reversed Eve's negation.

Let's move on to another prophecy, a comforting verse from the prophet Isaiah: 'Therefore the Lord himself will give you a sign. Behold, a virgin shall conceive, and bear a son, and shall call his name Emmanuel' (Is 7:14). The original Hebrew word *almah* in fact means a young woman, and not necessarily a virgin, but it is interesting that Jewish scholars who translated the Hebrew Bible into Greek – and who obviously knew their Hebrew – actually translated this Hebrew word as 'virgin' (*parthenos*). This translation makes sense of the context, because if a virgin conceives a child, this exceptional event is more likely to be regarded as a divine sign than simply a young woman doing so (the latter is the norm and so unremarkable). The Gospel of Matthew quotes from this Greek translation of the Hebrew Bible that was put together by Jewish scholars and Matthew also uses the term 'virgin' in his quotation. In relation to Mary, this prophecy has been understood through the centuries as a sign of her virginal integrity and of the divine origin of her son, the future Messiah.

In this prophecy, Mary's son is called Emmanuel, a Hebrew word meaning 'God with us'. As it turned out, he didn't actually receive this name, since the angel Gabriel instructed Mary to call her son Jesus, and not Emmanuel. Yet these names complement one another, because together they tell us two crucial things about Mary's son. First, in the person of his son, God saves (the literal meaning of the name Jesus), and second, in the person of Jesus, God is with us (Emmanuel). Indeed, in his parting words to his disciples in the Gospel of Matthew, Jesus tells them that he will always be Emmanuel for them: 'I am with you always, even to the end of the age' (Mt 28:20).

Another beautiful prophecy that points to Mary is found in the prophet Micah: 'But you, Bethlehem Ephratah, though you are small among the clans of Judah, out of you will come for me one who will be ruler over Israel, whose origins are from of old, from ancient times. Therefore he will give them up, until the time that she who labours has brought forth' (Mic 5:2–3). The religious leaders of Jesus' time were familiar with this prophecy. When Herod the Great asks the chief priests and teachers of the law where the Messiah is to be born, they tell him it is in Bethlehem, and support what they say by quoting Micah. In Hebrew, the word Bethlehem means 'house of bread', and this place name is especially appropriate for the one who is to be the bread of life. The word Ephratah means fruitful. The area around Bethlehem was fertile, full of sheep grazing on its pastures: 'There were shepherds living out in the fields nearby, keeping watch over their flocks at night' (Lk 2:8). But in a deeper way, Jesus, the fruit of her womb, is the Saviour whose life is fruitful for all, and who invites everyone to bear fruit, fruit that will last.

Poor yet chosen

Mary lived in Nazareth, only a few miles from the booming cosmopolitan city of Sepphoris. Nazareth was very much an ordinary town, a town that was overlooked and looked down upon: 'can anything good come out of Nazareth?' (Jn 1:46). Sepphoris, on the other hand, was affluent and prosperous. Perched on a hill, it had a Roman theatre that could accommodate 3,000 spectators. Sepphoris is never mentioned in the New Testament, so we have no record of Jesus ever having visited this city, only an hour's walk from Nazareth. Jesus preferred to spend time with ordinary folk.

Mary was one of these simple folk herself, even though she was chosen to bear God's Son out of all the women on earth: 'Do not be afraid, Mary, for you have found favour with God' (Lk 1:30). To say that Mary was chosen doesn't mean she was prominent or well-known. When God chose the Jewish nation it was anything but an economic powerhouse or a military superpower. In fact it was a relatively unknown nation. As for Mary, she was even more obscure. But that suited God fine, because as a rule he is drawn to those who are lowly and of little standing in the eyes of the world. God's reasoning goes against our all-too-human way of thinking: 'It was not because you are more numerous than all the peoples that the Lord has set his heart on you and chosen you; for you are really the smallest of all peoples' (Deut 7:7). If the Jewish people had been a powerful nation before God chose them, any success they achieved later would inevitably have been attributed to their own ingenuity and resources. However, because they were 'really the smallest of all peoples', their later achievements clearly reflected God's greatness. The primacy of God is reflected in what has over time become the key event in Jewish history: the liberation of the Hebrew people from their oppression and slavery in Egypt.

Just as the sense of being chosen is foundational to Jewish identity, so too it was central to Mary's sense of herself. Mary felt chosen, and not on account of any inherent greatness, for she was spiritually poor and she knew it: 'For he has looked upon the lowliness of his servant' (Lk 1:48). Mary knew that the greatness belonged to God: 'the Almighty has done great things for me' (Lk 1:49). Mary was one of the *anawim*, a Hebrew term used in the Bible to designate the poor. The biblical term *anawim* is not limited to the materially poor, but refers especially to those who are humble, lowly, detached from worldly ways, and utterly given to God.

The prophet Zephaniah predicted a future where the faithful poor would stand out for their trust in God. 'On that day you, Jerusalem, will not be put to shame for all the wrongs you have done to me, because I will remove from you your arrogant boasters. Never again will you be haughty on my holy mountain. But I will leave within you the meek and humble. The remnant of Israel will trust in the name of the Lord' (Zeph 3:11–12). All the hopes of Israel would be kept alive and concentrated in this tiny remnant of the *anawim*.

Zephaniah called upon the daughter of Zion and the daughter of Jerusalem to rejoice at this stirring promise: 'Sing, Daughter of Zion; shout aloud, Israel! Be glad and rejoice with all your heart, Daughter of Jerusalem! (Zeph 3:14). The daughter of Zion refers to the faithful remnant who continue to show trust and confidence in God. Mary, in her total surrender to God, represents the daughter of Zion in a sterling way. The prophet Zephaniah addressed as the daughter of Zion the small remnant that had returned from exile in Babylon, and had been purified through this trying experience. These survivors were now ready to recognise God as their true king. In this new joy, they would rebuild the Temple at Jerusalem, and God would return to live in the midst of his people. Mary personifies this new dawn of hope: in her God would come to live in the new Ark of the Covenant and in the new Temple, no longer made of stone, but now pulsing and alive.

Mary lived in total dependence upon the God who had brought her people out of Egypt through his saving power. As one of the *anawim* of God, Mary recalled and treasured God's saving actions, not only in the history of her people but in her own story as well. God had led her impoverished and exiled people through the wilderness to the Promised Land, and Mary experienced the liberating action of God in her life too. She realised her own nothingness, but that realisation alone wasn't what made her so startlingly humble. The foundation and source of Mary's humility was her reverence for God. It was because Mary was so deeply aware of the contrast between God and herself that she was so humble. Mary clearly saw the gulf between God's immeasurable greatness and her own insignificance.

Mary could authentically take the lowest place because she glimpsed God's utter perfection more clearly than the rest of us do. She knew that God wanted everything from her, and that's what she gave him. Her whole being incarnated the very heart of Jewish belief, expressed in the first part of the famous prayer *Shema Yisra'el* (Hear, Israel) from the Book of Deuteronomy: 'Hear, Israel, the Lord is our God, the Lord is One. And you shall love the Lord your God with all your heart and with all your soul and with all your strength. And these words that I command you today shall be in your heart. And you shall teach them diligently to your children, and you shall speak of them when you sit at home, and when you walk along the way, and when you lie down and when you rise up' (Deut 6:4–7).

The spirituality of Mary or way of the *anawim* received a new impetus with the Second Vatican Council (1962–65). In the written documents of the council, the Church was no longer presented in a triumphalist way, but instead as a community at the service of the entire world. The

Council Fathers did not declare any anathemas and did not condemn anyone. They humbly acknowledged that the Church does 'not always have a ready answer to every question' (*Gaudium et Spes* 33). They made it clear that 'the Church, although it needs human resources to carry out its mission, is not set up to seek earthly glory, but to proclaim, even by its own example, humility and self-sacrifice' (*Lumen Gentium* 8). They emphasised the positive elements in other world faiths and opened the Church up to dialogue. For instance, with reference to Judaism, they highlighted a common spiritual heritage and encouraged 'mutual understanding and respect which is the fruit, above all, of biblical and theological studies as well as of fraternal dialogues' (*Nostra Aetate* 4).

They highlighted Mary as someone whose only wealth was her huge trust in God, alluding to her as one of the *anawim*: 'She stands out among the poor and humble of the Lord, who confidently hope for and receive salvation from him. With her the exalted Daughter of Sion, and after a long expectation of the promise, the times are fulfilled' (*Lumen Gentium* 55).

Recent popes have placed Mary among the humble ones. In his General Audience of 23 May 2001, while commenting on Psalm 149, Pope John Paul II said: 'With such confidence the "sons of Zion" (v. 2), the *hasidim* and *anawim*, the faithful and the poor, go on to live their witness in the world and in history. Mary's canticle in the Gospel of Luke, the Magnificat, is the echo of the best sentiments of the "sons of Zion": glorious praise of God her Saviour, thanksgiving for the great things done by the Mighty One, the battle against the forces of evil, solidarity with the poor and fidelity to the God of the Covenant.'

On 15 February 2006, Pope Benedict XVI once again connected the spirituality of the *anawim* to Mary. Speaking of Mary's Magnificat at his General Audience, he said: 'It is a canticle that reveals in filigree the spirituality of the biblical *anawim*, that is, of those faithful who not only recognise themselves as "poor" in the detachment from all idolatry of riches and power, but also in the profound humility of a heart emptied of the temptation to pride and open to the bursting in of the divine saving grace.'

In his message for World Youth Day 2014, Pope Francis spoke of the *anawim* and singled out Mary's Magnificat as the rallying call for this spirituality: 'The first Beatitude, our theme for the next World Youth Day, says that the poor in spirit are blessed for theirs is the kingdom of heaven… First of all, let us try to understand what it means to be "poor in spirit … The Greek adjective *ptochós* (poor) does not have a purely material meaning. It means "a beggar", and it should be seen as linked to the Jewish notion of the *anawim*, "God's poor". It suggests lowliness, a sense of one's limitations and existential poverty. The *anawim* trust in the Lord, and they know that they can count on him… Dear friends, the Magnificat, the Canticle of Mary, poor in spirit, is also the song of everyone who lives by the Beatitudes. The joy of the Gospel arises from a heart which, in its poverty, rejoices and marvels at the works of God, like the heart of Our Lady, whom all generations call "blessed".'

Each of these three popes – John Paul II, Benedict XVI and Francis – mentions the Magnificat as an example of the spirituality of the *anawim*. Moreover, they suggest that the core of the Magnificat is its celebration of God's love for the *anawim*.

Mary's Jewish identity

Mary's profile acquires sharper relief if we look at her in terms of her Jewish identity. As this chapter has elucidated, a vital part of Mary's Jewish identity can be found through exploring Marian signs in the Old Testament. If we limit ourselves to looking at Mary through New Testament eyes, we won't glimpse her true depth. So much of her richness only begins to make sense when we acquire a basic familiarity with key figures and themes in the Old Testament. Saint Augustine said that the New Testament is hidden in the Old Testament, while the Old Testament is fulfilled in the New Testament. Since the New Testament is *hidden* in the Old Testament, we shouldn't expect it to jump out immediately before our eyes: we need to do some digging in order to uncover it.

We can discern this hidden meaning if we go beyond interpreting the Bible in a merely literal way. If we insist on sticking to the literal meaning, we won't get to the spiritual heart of Holy Scripture. We need to be brave enough to use our imagination. To imagine is *not* to invent; it is to 'see' with the mind something that is not immediately evident. For instance, with our imagination we can see the connection between Eve and Mary. To imagine is *not* to escape into fantasy or dreaminess, but to enlarge our vision of reality. For instance, with our imagination we can enlarge our way of envisaging Mary by associating her with images and symbols from the Old Testament. To imagine is to discover connections between things that initially seem disconnected. For instance, it is to discover a connection between Mary and the Ark of the Covenant.

Since the New Testament is hidden in the Old, it takes time to peel away the layers of concealment. The Second Vatican Council counsels patience: we won't see the connections all at once. 'The books of the Old Testament describe the history of salvation, by which the coming of Christ into the world was slowly prepared. These earliest documents, as they are read in the Church and are understood in the light of a further and full revelation, bring the figure of the woman, Mother of the Redeemer, into a gradually clearer light' (*Lumen Gentium*, 55).

As a final example of how to put the Old Testament into dialogue with the figure of Mary, while also expanding the dialogue into a three-way conversation or 'trialogue', let's look at the dogma of the Assumption, which traces its roots to the Old Testament, but is also linked in a moving way with Jewish identity in the wake of the Holocaust or Shoah.

A word first on dogma, which is a teaching of the Church that is divinely revealed. Unfortunately, dogma has become a bad word for many people. Bishops and priests are partially to blame for this negativity, because we've often presented dogmas in a rigid and inflexible way. The way I look at it, a dogma isn't a road sign that says 'stop'. It's more like rounding a bend on a country road and seeing an awe-inspiring panorama. As the American writer Flannery O'Connor said, 'a dogma is only a gateway to contemplation and is an instrument of freedom and not of restriction'. A dogma opens us up to a mystery so deep we can never plumb its depths, but only contemplate it again and again.

The dogma of the Assumption is a dogma about one of the biggest issues anyone has to face: the value of human life. Do human beings have value? Are their lives worth living? Does everything end with death? And if not, what is there after death? The dogma was proclaimed in 1950, five years after the value of human life was shaken by some of the most horrific questions ever raised. World War II, the deadliest war in history, ended in 1945, with the estimated deaths of up to eighty-five million people. Among the victims were six million Jews, many of whom died in atrocious circumstances, after terrible abuse and torture.

The dogma of the Assumption is a teaching about a Jewish woman, Mary of Nazareth. This fact is hugely significant in the context of the annihilation of millions of Jewish lives before and during the Second World War. The dogma of the Assumption teaches that at the end of her earthly existence, Mary was taken up body and soul into the glory of heaven. (Whereas Jesus ascended to heaven through his own power – hence the Ascension, Mary was raised to heaven through God's power – hence the Assumption.) This is an unambiguous answer to the disturbing questions about human dignity raised by the destruction and bloodshed of the Second World War. The fact that Mary is fully taken up into heaven is a clear endorsement of the inviolable dignity of every human life, especially every Jewish life.

Even if the powerful and unjust trample the downtrodden underfoot, God has counted every one of their tears. Even if their arms are branded with dehumanising numbers in concentration camps, God knows each one of their names. In God's eyes, the victims of suffering and injustice are never forgotten. The dogma that Mary is in heavenly glory is an encouragement for us who are still on our pilgrim way on earth: those who trust in God will not be disappointed.

In scriptural terms, the Assumption of Mary begins to make sense when we turn to the Old Testament. The second chapter of the Second Book of Kings tells us that the towering prophet Elijah was taken up in a whirlwind to heaven. The fifth chapter of the Book of Genesis tells us that Enoch, the great-grandfather of Noah, after walking with God during his life, was also taken up by God into heaven. If Enoch and Elijah were assumed into heaven, all the more reason this should be Mary's sublime destiny. After all, the angel Gabriel greeted her as 'full of grace', and her cousin Elizabeth, filled with the Holy Spirit, praised her as 'blessed among women'.

Mary is profoundly Jewish. She's not a threat to anyone. She is a promise, the promise of our own glorious future. Despite all the small and big tragedies of our lives, we are not heading for ultimate destruction. A blessedness beyond compare awaits us. And in the midst of that heavenly glory, Mary already awaits us.

CHAPTER FOUR

MARY *and* ISLAM

*The angels said to Mary: 'Mary, God has chosen you and made you
pure: He has truly chosen you above all women'.*
The Qur'an (3:42)

The first part of this chapter looks at how the Qur'an portrays the
figure of Mary (called by her Arabic name, *Mariyam*). It turns out that
Mary is depicted in an astoundingly positive way, as a virgin who is the
embodiment of virtue and a model for others to emulate. At the same
time, there is a crucial difference – the Qur'an doesn't see Mary as the
Mother of God. This is because Islam believes that Jesus (called *Isa*), even
though he is born of the Virgin Mary (yes, Muslims believe in the virgin
birth) and is a great prophet, is nevertheless only human. Perhaps because
Jesus is given a much lower place in Islam than in Christianity, Mary is
given a correspondingly higher place.

The Qur'an has a different 'take' on the story of Mary, and so invites
us to picture her in new ways. And some of these new ways turn out to
be surprisingly familiar. Take Mary's Presentation in the Temple, a feast
that Catholic and Orthodox Christians celebrate on 21 November each
year. Although there is no mention of this event in the Bible, the Qur'an
describes how Mary was brought to the Temple and spent her childhood
years there. However, although Mary's presentation in the Temple doesn't
figure in the Bible, it is important to note that there is an account of it
in the Protoevangelium of James, a work that reflects the beliefs of many
early Christians.

In the second part of this chapter, I ask how Mary can help in the
dialogue between Christians and Muslims. Through reflecting upon
Mary's story in the Qur'an and through asking about her role in our
dialogue with Muslims, we can go beyond a predictable and jaded way
of looking at her. It's astounding to think that a humble Jewish woman
from two thousand years ago could enhance the relationship between
the world's two biggest religions of today – Christianity and Islam. This

realisation could save us from our small and sometimes reductive images of this woman from Nazareth.

Mary in the Qur'an

Catholics and, indeed, all Christians are usually surprised to discover how positively the Virgin Mary is depicted in the Qur'an. She is the only woman mentioned by name in this book that is so sacred to Muslims. Other women in the Qur'an are known as 'the wife of Adam' or 'Pharaoh's wife', and so on, but not by their own names. Mary is the exception. She is mentioned by name over thirty times: that's more often than her name appears in the New Testament. Moreover, one chapter (*surah*) of the Qur'an, chapter nineteen, is dedicated especially to her. It is called *Surah Mariyam*, or the 'surah of Mary'. The Qur'an practically overflows in its praise for Mary. It teaches that she was chosen from all women, purified by God, born miraculously, already consecrated to God while in the womb, preserved from Satan's grasp, presented to God in the Temple, a virgin par excellence, truthful, devout, obedient and prayerful.

However, despite the effusive portrayal of Mary in the Qur'an, it has not led to a passionate enthusiasm for her among Muslims: a genuine respect certainly, but not a fervent devotion. There is a contrast between the praise that the Qur'an lavishes upon Mary, and the relative unfamiliarity of most ordinary Muslims with this woman who is so celebrated by their holy book. Mary is certainly not foreign to Muslims – she is mentioned so often in the Qur'an that it would be impossible not to have some awareness of her. But beyond a basic acquaintance with Mary, many Muslims don't know a lot about her.

This clear discrepancy between the positive written words about Mary in the Qur'an and the more muted devotion to her among Muslims may appear puzzling to us. How come they haven't put the Qur'an's praise of Mary into practice in their way of living their faith? But that is to forget that we Christians also have similar gaps between things that are clear in scripture but which we do not take on board in our daily lives. For instance, we're often reluctant to face up to the truth that Jesus was Jewish. As a result, we separate Jesus from the whole context in which he was born and reared. Here is an example of how this lack of awareness of the Jewishness of Jesus affects us: when Christians go on pilgrimage to the Holy Land, they often visit the ruins of old synagogues, but rarely enter a functioning one. Yet Jesus himself didn't hang around synagogues that had fallen into disrepair, but instead attended real synagogues where the faithful gathered to pray and to worship God. As part of our imitation of Jesus, it would make sense to have contact with the living Jewish faith, rather than just peering at derelict synagogues.

The Qur'an reveres Mary as a virgin and declares that she is the mother of Jesus. Yet there are significant differences between the picture it paints of Mary and what the Gospels tell us about her. These divergences are due above all to the fact that the Qur'an sees Jesus as human but not divine. Although Jesus is frequently called the son of Mary in the Qur'an, he is never called the Son of God. Jesus is revered as someone especially blessed by God, a prophet, teacher, a servant of God, a miracle worker and someone worthy of respect both in this world and in the next, but he is not seen as a Saviour. According to the Qur'an, Jesus did not die and so was not crucified. Before death, he was assumed into heaven on account of his holiness, and he will return in the end times to slay the Antichrist.

Since Jesus is not regarded as divine in Islam, Mary is not considered to be the mother of God. Yet this title – 'Mother of God' – is Mary's most significant title in Christianity. To express this somewhat differently, we can say that the most important way Christians have of describing Mary is totally absent in the Qur'an. Although Muslims show great reverence for Mary, ultimately they only venerate her as the mother of a great prophet. It could be argued that despite several common features in the portrayal of Mary in Christianity and Islam, each of our faiths is in fact using the same name – Mary – to depict two diffferent persons. But I believe that to claim we are talking about two different people when we talk about Mary is to claim too much. Both of our faiths agree on many virtues and personality traits that characterise Mary. Nonetheless, we should not underestimate or minimise this crucial difference – the fact that for us she is the Mother of God, but not for Muslims.

The Incarnation is the fundamental reason that the New Testament views Mary in such a different light from the Qur'an. Because Christians believe that the Son of God took flesh in Mary's womb, it makes sense to call her the Mother of God. Islam views things differently: no human being could be the mother of God; in fact, no creature could ever be close enough to God to be related to God as a mother, son or daughter. Just as it is inconceivable in their eyes that Mary could be the mother of God, so too it's unthinkable that any of us could call ourselves the children of God.

Muslims are convinced that the omnipotent and transcendent God would never take on human flesh. The notion that God would descend from his inaccessible holiness to become a human person is simply anathema to them. Christians, by contrast, believe that the Second Person of the Blessed Trinity lowered himself to adopt our human condition in all things but sin: the Word became flesh and dwelt among us. The fact that Muslims find the idea of the incarnation so improbable is a reminder to us as Christians of what an extraordinary privilege it is that our transcendent and omnipotent God has deigned to descend to our level. Too often we take this mind-boggling truth for granted.

Despite these crucial differences, the Qur'an can help us look at Mary with renewed warmth and reverence. Although the New Testament only takes up the story of Mary when she is already a young woman and betrothed to Joseph, the Qur'an tells her story from before she was born. In surah 3:35 of the Qur'an, Mary's mother (whose name is not given in the Qur'an, where she is only known as the wife of Imran) consecrates the child within her womb to God, in the hope that it will be a baby boy. She appears disappointed when she gives birth to a little girl. But, being a good Muslim, she surrenders herself to God's will, names the child Mary and places her under God's care, asking that she be protected from Satan. God responds graciously and blesses Mary so that she grows like a flourishing plant.

The Qur'an presents the young Mary as a beautiful and healthy child. The Gospels, on the other hand, have nothing to say about Mary's physical appearance. Even among Muslims of our own day, there is a widespread opinion that Mary was the most beautiful – and devout – woman of her time. Of course, the Qur'an portrays Mary's beauty as more than skin-deep: it is a matter of her whole personality and character.

The Qur'an's celebration of Mary's inner and outer beauty invites us as Christians to take seriously this appealing quality of Mary. It is a quality that is already intimated in our scripture and has also been praised by many Christian mystics. In the vision of the woman clothed with the sun from the twelfth chapter of the Book of Revelation, the beauty of a creature (the woman) is enveloped in the beauty of the divine (the sun). Mary's beauty has been even more clearly expressed by countless Christian mystics and believers over the centuries.

An ancient prayer from the fourth century gives lyrical expression to Mary's beauty: 'You are all beautiful, Mary. And the original stain is not in you' (*Tota pulchra es, Maria. Et macula originalis non est in Te*). In the fourteenth century, the Swedish mystic Saint Bridget said, 'There is no joy that does not grow from hers, nor any delight that is not completed by the vision of her beauty.' Closer to our own time, Saint Faustina Kowalska (1905–1938) wrote in her diary: 'O Mother, Virgin, most beautiful lily, your heart was for Jesus the first tabernacle on earth.'

Although the Qur'an draws our attention to the physical beauty of Mary, it is not fixated on her outer beauty. The beauty of Mary in the Qur'an is most of all the beauty of a life well lived. Beauty in this sense means completion or wholeness. According to a saying (*hadith*) attributed to the prophet Muhammad, Mary stands out as a spiritually perfected woman. The Catholic tradition would agree, locating Mary's beauty in the way she fulfilled her life's task and perfectly accomplished the mission that God had entrusted to her.

The Qur'an informs us that Mary's childhood years are spent in the Temple under the care of the priest Zechariah (who also features in the Gospel of Luke, though not as Mary's guardian). When she reaches her teenage years, she returns to her family. At this point, like other young women and men, she should prepare herself for marriage, as stipulated by the Qur'an itself. Instead, Mary does a surprising thing: according to surah 19:16 she moves away from her family to some unspecified eastern location. Mary has decided to renounce marriage in order to give herself completely to the worship and adoration of God. The Qur'an makes no mention of Joseph, but Muslim scholars inform us that he was a cousin of Mary and provided her with food and water during her retreat in the east.

The next pivotal moment is the announcement to Mary of her virginal conception. This is told twice, both in surah 3, where angels deliver the message, and in surah 19 where the message is transmitted by an angel in the form of a perfect man. The announcement is told from two different angles: surah 3 places the emphasis on Mary's own words, whereas surah 19 gives more attention to the angel's announcement. Let's put together what we are told in surah 3 and surah 19, starting with the latter.

When a person unknown to Mary (in reality an angel) approaches her in this isolated place, her reaction is predictably one of fear. She tells the stranger that she seeks refuge against him in the Lord, asking if he is a righteous person (surah 19:18). The stranger stresses that he is merely the messenger of God, with the mission of giving her a pure son (surah 19:18). In surah 3, Mary receives an extraordinary promise. The angels tell her that God brings her good news of a 'Word' from God himself, someone called the Messiah or 'Jesus, son of Mary'. He will be highly respected in this world and the world to come. He will already speak when he is in the cradle (surah 3:45–46). The angels tell Mary that everything is possible for God, since he has created all that there is from nothing by a simple command (3:47).

Initially when Mary is told that she will have a son, she asks how this can happen since she is a virgin and has resolved to remain a virgin (surah 19:20). The angel explains that this is easy for God to do. He adds that God will make Jesus a sign for the people and a bearer of mercy, adding that the matter has already been decided (19:21). What stands out in the Qur'an is Mary's no-holds-barred surrender to God. Although Mary does not say anything in reply, it is evident that she immediately obeys, for in the following verse we discover that she is carrying the child Jesus inside her, and has set herself apart in a remote place (19:22).

There is a crucial difference here between the Bible and the Qur'an, a difference that is easy to overlook. In the Bible, Mary verbally gives her assent. She says: 'Behold the handmaid of the Lord, be it done unto me according to thy word.' These words indicate a knowing, responsible and free acceptance of God's request. However, in the Qur'an, things are different: in the holy book of Islam, Mary does not utter any words in response to the command from God that she is to bear a son. Since Islam views God as a master and not as a father, the expected response to God is submission. Despite the difference between submission in Islam and Christian surrender, we can learn something from the way Islam views Mary's obedience to God. It helps us to see how radical and complete Mary's act of surrender truly is. Through this act, Mary gives everything to God: her body and soul, her present and future.

As Christians, it helps us to see that, above all, Mary consecrates to God the gift of her free will. The rest of creation follows a predetermined path, but only human beings can say yes or no. This freedom makes us like God, and so free will really is a divine gift. Through her free will, Mary can determine the path she chooses and be mistress of her own destiny. God will not take this gift away from her, for he fully respects human freedom. Admittedly, we can grieve God through using our free will to refuse him, but also, thanks to this gift, we can love God as well. Through her prompt and unreserved obedience, Mary places this splendid gift at God's disposal.

In the Qur'an, labour pains come upon Mary next to a palm tree (19:23), in a location that isn't specified. In the New Testament, by contrast, Mary gives birth in a named place, Bethlehem (and moreover a name that is 'pregnant' with meaning – literally, 'house of bread'). Furthermore, in the Catholic tradition, Mary's act of giving birth has traditionally been regarded as free of labour pains. Indeed, the energy of Mary immediately after Jesus's birth may just indicate as much: 'she gave birth to her firstborn, a son; she wrapped him in cloths and placed him in a manger' (Lk 2:7). Mary's freedom from labour pains makes sense in the context of her exemption from the negative consequences of the fall of Adam and Eve. After their sin, God tells the woman that she will experience pain in giving birth (Gen 3:16). However, since Mary is free of original sin, this presumably does not apply to her.

In the Qur'an, Mary's family reacts badly when she arrives home carrying her newborn baby. They know that Mary is unmarried, and they presume she has done wrong. They remind her that her father was a good man and her mother was a chaste woman (19:28). God has instructed Mary to keep silent, so she does not defend herself. In any event, her words might not be believed. All she does is simply to point to her child Jesus. Her family is incredulous: how can any of them possibly conduct a meaningful conversation with an infant in a crib? But to the amazement of them all, and just as the angels had promised in surah 3:46, her baby starts speaking from the crib, and not just baby language, but intelligent and inspired words, defending his mother's honour, reputation and virginity.

The Qur'an praises Mary's virginity. However, this does not imply that virginity itself has an exalted place in Islam. Certainly it is valued as something that a woman brings to marriage, but not as a state in which a woman should remain. Muslim women are encouraged to marry, and not to remain virgins forever. Mary's virginity is commended, not so much on account of virginity itself, but because it is such a compelling sign of God's omnipotence. God is so powerful that he can reconcile two apparent opposites, by making a mother out of a virgin. God's power is utterly creative, and so his power in uniting motherhood and virginity in Mary is on a par with his power in creating Adam.

Once the Qur'an finishes telling the extraordinary episode of how her infant child mounts such an articulate defence of her, it has little to say about Mary. There is nothing about how she reared Jesus, there isn't a word about whether she had any role in his public life, and she isn't depicted as standing at the cross, because, according to the Qur'an, Jesus wasn't crucified. He only appeared to die. Being a prophet, the curse of being crucified would have been an insult to his dignity, and so instead God raised Jesus up to himself.

Mary and the relationship between Catholics and Muslims today

Having looked at what the Qur'an has to say about Mary, it is worth asking what role Mary could play in the relationship between Muslims and Catholics today. Since the early 1960s, the Catholic Church has emphasised the good qualities in Islam as well as highlighting the shared respect that both Catholics and Muslims show toward Mary. Indeed, since the historic document *Nostra Aetate* (also known by its official English title, *The Declaration on the Relation of the Church to Non-Christian Religions*) was promulgated on 28 October 1965, much has changed for the better in the long and troubled relationship between Catholics and Muslims. The positive effects of *Nostra Aetate* are still unfolding today, as it continues to transform our relationship with Muslims and those of other non-Christian faiths.

Nostra Aetate is by far the shortest of the Second Vatican Council's sixteen documents, with fewer than 1,200 words, yet arguably the document with the largest resonance of all. For with the publication of this document, Catholic teaching about non-Christian religions shifted overnight from being a teaching of disapproval and even censure to being a teaching of thoughtful respect. *Nostra Aetate* brought about a paradigm shift that would have been difficult to envisage in the early or even the mid-twentieth century.

Nostra Aetate notes: 'The Church has also a high regard for the Muslims ... Although not acknowledging him as God, they venerate Jesus as a prophet, his Virgin Mother they also honour, and even at times devoutly invoke.' (*Nostra Aetate* 3). During a visit to the Great Mosque of Damascus on 6 May, 2001, Pope John Paul II remarked: 'As we make our way through life towards our heavenly destiny, Christians feel the company of Mary, the mother of Jesus; and Islam too pays tribute to Mary and hails her as "chosen above the women of the world".' More recently, in *Evangelii Gaudium* (2013), Pope Francis remarked: 'The sacred writings of Islam have retained some Christian teachings; Jesus and Mary receive profound veneration ...' (*Evangelii Gaudium* 252).

Mary has an important role to play in the growing relationship between Catholics and Muslims. Moreover, Mary herself is a model for our dialogue, and for several reasons. She was ready to listen – and to respond – when God asked her to become the mother of Jesus. And so she embodied the spirit of respect in which the two-way communication of dialogue should be conducted. Additionally, she was flexible and adaptable enough to abandon her own plans and follow God's plan instead. Last but not least, she was a mother, and this gives her an appeal that transcends any particular culture or religion.

When it comes to dialogue, there are several different levels. Two documents issued by the Pontifical Council for Inter-Religious Dialogue, one in 1984, and the other in 1991, helpfully distinguish four levels of dialogue:

✛ The dialogue of life;
✛ The dialogue of action;
✛ The dialogue of theological exchange;
✛ The dialogue of religious experience.

The dialogue of life is where people live as good neighbours, giving each other a helping hand in the struggles of everyday existence. The dialogue of action is about working together to build a better and more just world. The dialogue of theological exchange is where scholars examine specialised questions to arrive at a deeper understanding of their respective traditions. The dialogue of religious experience is where people share their spiritual paths, their experiences of prayer and worship.

The dialogue of action needs to be prioritised in our present world situation. Since religion is so often used today as a justification for violence, Christians and Muslims need to build a better world together. Pope Francis himself agrees. He believes that the most urgent – and prophetic – type of dialogue today is the dialogue of action. During his visit to the United Arab Emirates in February 2019, he urged Christians and Muslims to 'build a future together or there will be no future'.

The dialogue of action is about working together for humanitarian goals, in order to foster human freedom and development in social, economic and political ways. To put this even more starkly: the dialogue of action is not about making joint declarations on world hunger, but about getting our hands dirty in order to *do* something about world hunger.

Christians and Muslims already share many moral and ethical values in common. The dialogue of action can build on this in an era when there are so many global and local problems that are crying out to be addressed.

Together we can achieve immeasurably more than we can do alone. The dialogue of action is truly prophetic: if we took it seriously, we could transform our world. In his book, *The Prophets*, Abraham Joshua Heschel describes the prophetic thirst for justice with these stirring words: 'To us the moral state of society, for all its stains and spots, seems fair and trim; to the prophet it is dreadful ... Our standards are modest; our sense of injustice tolerable, timid; our moral indignation impermanent; yet human violence is interminable, unbearable, permanent. To us life is often serene, in the prophet's eye the world reels in confusion.'

Mary is a model for Catholics and Christians in the dialogue of action for a number of reasons. First, she was sensitive to injustice and oppression as the Magnificat makes clear. Second, she was faithful to those in suffering as is shown by the fact that she stood by Jesus at the Cross. Third, she was a unifying force in the midst of the apostles as they gathered in prayer to invoke the Holy Spirit in the days leading up to Pentecost.

When it comes to Muslims, Mary can also be a model for them in the dialogue of action, first, because she is such a prominent woman in the Qur'an (the only woman mentioned by name in the entire book), second, because the Qur'an shows her immediate willingness to do what God wanted done, and third, because the Qur'an shows how she herself was excluded and marginalised, with the result that she can empathise deeply with anyone in difficulty.

Although the relationship between Catholics and Muslims has improved since *Nostra Aetate* was promulgated on 28 October 1965, there is still a long road to travel. Just over half a century has elapsed since then. Psalm 90, verse 4, tells us that: 'A thousand years in your sight are like a day that has just gone by, or like a watch in the night'. If a thousand years are like a day – twenty-four hours – in God's sight, what is half a century like? A little over an hour! We have had a little over an hour of a positive relationship, so we ought not to be too hasty in drawing enormously optimistic conclusions from our relatively satisfying sixty or so minutes together.

Over the centuries, Christians and Muslims learned to see each other with suspicious eyes, and changing a world view is no easy task. There are few things that become so stubbornly entrenched as the vantage point from which we make sense of everything. A world view, like a filter, lets through certain images but blocks others. While we view the world through our preferred lens, we easily forget that it is not the only lens.

Yet despite the dark days of the past, we have an opportunity to live in a new moment of light. I pray that this light will become brighter, and that mutual understanding and respect will flourish. I hope that we Catholics and Muslims will learn to value the shared treasure we have in Mary – or Mariyam, as she is called in the Qur'an. May the example of her exquisite kindness help us to abandon polemics and hostility, and replace them instead with a spirit of mutual respect. May we learn, like Mary, to think and speak the language of compassion.

CHAPTER FIVE

UNIVERSAL RELEVANCE
and INDIVIDUAL APPEAL

Because you are there always, just because you are Mary, just because you exist, Mother of Jesus Christ, receive our thanks.
Paul Claudel

Different Traditions

There have been many disagreements, divisions and even wars between the world's religions over the last two thousand years. Within Christianity itself, the last millennium has been especially difficult. The West and the East officially parted ways in 1054, and five hundred years later the Reformation unfolded, resulting in many different denominations.

Happily, the role of Mary did not contribute to the schism between the West and the East. In contrast, disagreements about Mary sadly figured in the disputes that took place at the time of the Reformation and afterwards.

On the one hand, the Reformers took issue with what they considered excessive veneration of Mary. But on the other hand, they still wanted to honour her. They can teach us Catholics of today to root our beliefs about Mary in the rich and fertile ground of the Bible. Saint Jerome, the fourth-century saint who translated most of the Bible into Latin, famously said that 'ignorance of Scripture is ignorance of Christ'. The love of the Reformed Churches for the Bible can help us realise that unfamiliarity with the Bible (the Old Testament as well as the New) leaves us with an impoverished understanding of Mary.

Orthodox Christianity remained outside the debates and quarrels about the Virgin Mary that embroiled the churches in the West from the time of the Reformation onwards. While bitter disputes raged between Catholics and Protestants, the Orthodox held on to an age-old Marian piety that stayed serenely rooted in the Church Fathers of the early centuries, and through them, in Scripture itself.

The Orthodox Churches have never added any new teachings since the time of the schism between East and West. Instead they have kept faithful to the teachings of the first millennium, when Christians formed a single and undivided Church. Because of this, their devotion to Mary has remained the same for two thousand years; so, for instance, there is no division between Mary's role in the liturgy and her role in popular Orthodox piety. In fact, popular Orthodox piety towards Mary is expressed in a special way in the liturgy.

It is tempting to dismiss tradition as a weight from the past that puts an obstacle in the way of progress. The Orthodox world points to a more liberating meaning of tradition: it is the wisdom of the past that can still be woven into the tapestry of the present. By staying loyal to their long-standing devotion to Mary, the Orthodox Churches do not feel chained to an outdated past. Instead, this devotion deepens their sense of who they are today. It gives them an anchored sense of identity.

The Orthodox Churches don't want to neglect Mary because they don't want to lose sight of an essential dimension of who they are and always have been. They show us that a love of Mary which is deeply rooted in the past can nevertheless still communicate a vision of goodness for our own day.

Just as we cannot adequately understand Jesus if we do not pay attention to his Jewish roots, so too we cannot properly appreciate Mary if we ignore the fact that she was Jewish. Mary is the high point in a long line of devout Jews who said yes to God. Her humble description of herself as the 'handmaid of the Lord' reminds us of the chosen people's sense of itself as belonging to God and having no other gods before him. Her Magnificat echoes the praises of numerous prophetic voices who thanked God for his mercy to Abraham and his descendants. Elizabeth, another Jewish woman, addresses Mary as the Mother of her Lord and as blessed among women, showing that Mary is the woman towards whom the matriarchs, heroines and prophets of the Jewish people point. In the prayers of the Catholic Church, we attribute to Mary some of the great religious symbols of Judaism, such as the Ark of the Covenant.

Even though our Jewish brothers and sisters cannot agree with our Marian way of reading the Old Testament, I hope they'll see it as a sign of our esteem and gratitude towards them for giving this amazing woman to the world. For this, we should be always grateful to them.

Many Catholics are unaware of how warmly Mary is portrayed in the Qur'an. We could benefit from becoming more familiar with the exceptional and privileged position that the holy book of Islam gives to the Virgin Mary. According to the Qur'an, Mary is favoured in a special way, purified by the express intervention of God, a virgin yet also a mother, chosen out of all the women in the world. However, Muslims do not share our Christian conviction that Mary is the Mother of God. Without denying our differences, we can nevertheless find in the Virgin Mary a rationale for working together. Our shared veneration for this outstanding woman is an encouragement to leave aside our long-lasting resentments and work for a better future in which she can delight.

Global Reach and Personal Appeal

The Virgin Mary has touched more people than any other woman in history, and for many reasons. She symbolises maternal love. She is an accessible avenue to God. She understands suffering. She knows the meaning of sacrifice. Catherine de Hueck Doherty, a refugee from the Russian Revolution who served the poor of Toronto and New York, expressed it like this: 'She possesses the secret of prayer, the secret of wisdom, for she is the Mother of God. Who else can teach you to burn with the fire of love except the Mother of fair love? Who else can teach you to pray except the woman of prayer? Who else can teach you to go through the silence of deserts and nights, the silence of pain and sorrow, the solitude of joy and gladness, except the woman wrapped in silence?'

Although Mary spoke only a handful of times in the New Testament, her personality and character have spoken to countless believers ever since, and not only to Catholics. Mary draws millions of people to shrines across the world. In addition to well-known shrines such as Guadalupe, Lourdes and Fatima, there are many other Marian shrines around the world that attract believers of other faiths.

Each year millions of devotees – Catholic, Hindu, Muslim and Zoroastrian – travel to the Basilica of Our Lady of Velankanni in Pakistan to ask for her help and intercession. In Odisha, eastern India, Our Lady appeared to a Hindu woman in 1994 and told her to ask the local Catholic priest to build a church on the mountain of Partama; Catholics and Hindus continue to flock to this site even on normal days. At some times during the year, almost as many Muslims as Christians come to the Shrine of Our Lady of Lebanon in the village of Harissa, near Beirut. On the island of Mindanao in the Philippines, many Muslims go to the shrine of Our Lady of Pilar, especially in times of difficulty or before undertaking their pilgrimage to Mecca.

These are just a few examples to show that devotion to Mary is a global phenomenon. She has so many different facets to her – from the young virgin in Nazareth to the grieving mother at Calvary – that there is always something appealing about her, whatever one's faith or lack of it. We yearn for a faith that is personal and engaging, for a faith that can become an intrinsic part of the rhythm of our everyday existence; and that is why the figure of Mary has come alive for countless believers. As Pope Francis puts it in his disarmingly informal way: 'She is my Mum' (*ella es mi Mamá*).

I have explored experiences, stories and images of Mary across several faith traditions, because a merely intellectual approach would never reveal what is at the core of Mary's faith: the love of God given and received. That is what Mary's life was about: a yes in reply to a love beyond all her dreams of love. Mary made a decision in response to a gift. She received the gift of an encounter with God who drew so near to her that the human flesh of his only-begotten Son was knitted together in her womb. At the heart of Mary's life was this love story with God, a love story that ideally can be at the heart of our lives as well.

Like any good mother, Mary gets us in touch with the affective dimension of our lives, and frees us up to be receptive to God. The first step to God is not a matter of theory. Neither is it an exercise in willpower alone. More often it's about opening up the basic flow of our lives so that we are ready to move towards trust, goodness and love. We easily get stuck in tired ways of doing things. But encountering the depth of Mary is a humbling invitation to live out of the depths of ourselves. She helps us to go deeper than our surface selves, and to anchor ourselves in a rootedness that goes back through the generations to Abraham and Sarah, and even predates them. She helps us to see what marvels the Almighty has done for us. She enables us to rejoice in God our Saviour.

SELECT BIBLIOGRAPHY

Best, Isabel (ed.). *The Collected Sermons of Dietrich Bonhoeffer*. Translated by Douglas W. Stott, Anne Schmidt-Lange, Isabel Best, Scott A. Moore, and Claudia D. Bergmann. Minneapolis, MN: Fortress Press, 2012.

Bethge, Eberhard *Dietrich Bonhoeffer: a biography* (Revised and edited by Victoria J. Barnett). Minneapolis, MN: Fortress Press, 2000.

Bonhoeffer, Dietrich. *Letters and Papers from Prison*. Translated by Reginald H. Fuller. London: SCM Press, 1953.

De La Potterie, Ignace. *Mary in the Mystery of the Covenant*. Translated by Bertrand Buby. New York, NY: Alba House, 1992.

Florovsky, Georges. *Creation and Redemption*, Belmont, MA: Nordland Publishing Company, 1976.

Gambero, Luigi. *Mary and the Fathers of the Church: The Blessed Virgin Mary in Patristic Thought*. Translated by Thomas Buffer. San Francisco, CA: Ignatius Press, 1999.

Kierkegaard, Søren. *Two Ages: The Age of Revolution and the Present Age: A Literary Review*. Translated by Howard V. Hong and Edna H. Hong. Princeton, NJ: Princeton University Press, 1978.

Kierkegaard, Søren. *Fear and Trembling*. Translated by Alastair Hannay. London: Penguin Books, 1985.

Kierkegaard, Søren. *For Self-Examination*. Translated by Howard V. Hong and Edna H. Hong. Princeton, NJ: Princeton University Press, 1990.

Pelikan, Jaroslav (ed.). *Luther's Works, Volume 21: The Sermon on the Mount and the Magnificat*. Saint Louis, MO: Concordia Publishing House, 1956.

Speake, Graham. *Mount Athos: Renewal in Paradise*. New Haven, CT, and London: Yale University Press, 2004.

The New American Bible (Revised Edition). New York, NY: HarperCollins, 2012.

The Qur'an. Translated by M.A.S. Abdel Haleem. New York, NY, and Oxford: Oxford University Press, 2005.

Wybrew, Hugh. *The Orthodox Liturgy: the Development of the Eucharistic Liturgy in the Byzantine Rite*. Crestwood, New York, NY: St Vladimir's Seminary Press, 1990.

Zander, Valentine. *St. Seraphim of Sarov*. Translated by Sister Gabriel Anne. London: SPCK, 1975.